THE GOTHICK TASTE

The Gothick Taste

Terence Davis

DAVID & CHARLES

NEWTON ABBOT · LONDON · VANCOUVER

0 7153 6697 1

Set in Monotype Baskerville
and printed in Great Britain
by Fletcher & Son Ltd, Norwich
for David & Charles (Holdings) Limited
South Devon House Newton Abbot Devon

Published in Canada by Douglas, David & Charles Limited
3645 Philips Drive West Vancouver BC

Designed by John Leath

For Nicolas

Contents

List of Illustrations

DRAWINGS IN THE TEXT

Acknowledgements

Many people have been kind enough to help me in gathering material for this essay and others have checked several of my wayward ideas on a wayward subject. In the former category I would like to thank particularly Mr John Harris, the Knight of Glin, Mr John Cornforth, Miss Dorothy Stroud, Mr Guy Acloque, Mr Howard Colvin and Mr John Harthan. In the latter, I am grateful for the initial encouragement and guidance of Sir John Summerson and Dr David Watkin and for critical help from Dr Alistair Rowan. To Dr J. Mordaunt Crook, whose introduction to the new edition of Eastlake has proved invaluable, I am indebted for reading my typescript and correcting some of my worst errors of fact and judgement.

Miss Philippa Lewis patiently found many of the illustrations and Mr Oliver Nares drew the plans.

TERENCE DAVIS

Covent Garden
London
1974

'I LEFT THE MANTLING SHADE IN MORAL MOOD —
SIGH'D AS THE MOULD'RING MONUMENTS I VIEWED.'

John Cunningham (1766)

'Elegy on a Pile of Ruins'
from *Poems Chiefly Pastoral*

Preface

Just over one hundred years ago Charles L. Eastlake published *A History of the Gothic Revival*. In 1928 Lord Clark's *Gothic Revival* first appeared. Since then Eastlake has been re-issued and contains a detailed and illuminating introduction by its editor, Dr J. Mordaunt Crook. Both Eastlake and Clark are standard works and a part of each is devoted to the eighteenth-century gothicists – the main subject of this essay.

Much has been written about this aspect of the Revival in varying degrees of tolerance, championship, dismissal and analysis according to personal taste, fashion and scholarship, and it now seems clear that the intentions of these gothicists have often been misinterpreted. This essay aims to be a selective, visual compendium of that particular fanciful evocation of the Middle Ages, mostly Rococo in spirit, that threaded its way through ten decades, finally to be lost in a tide of passionate loyalty to medieval architecture allied to a deep religious faith. It considers examples of the two main expressions of the Gothick-manifestation: its use as a form of decoration in its Rococo phase and its use to evoke a mood in its associational phase. Sometimes these phases overlap or are combined in unequal proportions, and the style, being what it is, embraces many aberrations in between, difficult to classify by any established architectural term.

In an attempt to limit repetition, unless quoting from sources I have used the word 'Gothick' to denote Georgian Gothic and the word 'Gothic' when referring to medieval forms. 'Gothic Revival' refers to the Victorian Gothic Revival.

In order to isolate the subject as far as possible, I have tried to place emphasis on the mid to late eighteenth century, the period when the style established itself reasonably clearly from what preceded it and the more eclectic phase that followed. It is the contagious, long-lasting Rococo element that I hope will stand out from the inexhaustible mass of complicated, interwoven and often conflicting material. In an essay of this scope it would not be possible to pursue, other than in outline, such topics as the Picturesque Movement or give detailed descriptions of important buildings, but I have referred the reader to authoritative sources on such subjects in notes for each chapter. Neither have I mentioned more than a handful of the host of follies so beautifully assembled by Miss Barbara Jones in her *Follies and Grottoes* (1953). Lack of balance is due to the nature of the subject and my inability to distil it more fairly.

The eighteenth-century gothicists have been accused, especially by the Victorians, of 'poor imitation' of ancient buildings but to do so is to entirely miss the point. They never said, in effect: 'Come and see my medieval castle', but rather, 'Come and see my house which might *remind* you of a medieval castle.' In their way they were quite honest about it. Although they occasionally adapted medieval detail reasonably accurately there was no question of slavish imitation, 'adapted' being the operative word, for even many of Horace Walpole's interior features were not strict copies but adaptations. And he admits in his own description of Strawberry Hill that 'the design of the chimney-piece is taken from the tomb of Edward the Confessor, improved by Mr Adam'. Their buildings were comfortable, modern and elegant variations on a theme, the imagination freed from the bondage of the Orders and the disciplinarian hand of Palladianism. They were expressing what Mr Christopher Hussey called 'impatience with the solemnly dull'. Once these facts are accepted, the Georgian gothicists can be better understood and appreciated.

When, by 1750, the conventional play with a limited vocabulary of Gothic patterns was scorned, the efforts of Walpole, James Wyatt and others, however different, were hardly more realistic, although Wyatt's grasp of Gothic techniques was masterly. They were more skilful and enterprising, sometimes more exciting and romantic, but no more 'authentic'. The style was an exotic daydream sometimes darkened by the nightmare qualities found in literature.

In this essay the buildings fall roughly into three main categories: shining examples such as Strawberry Hill, Arbury Hall and Fonthill Abbey which, because of their importance, I have given prominence; lesser houses that help to illustrate the development of the style in some of its more modest and capricious forms; landscapes adornments which all speak the same language. Church architecture is represented by some of its Gothic Survival, Rococo and Regency buildings. I have also glanced at furniture in order to give some idea of the style's endless vagaries.

The problem of selecting from this vast and rich quarry must, inevitably, mean the exclusion of favourite buildings and, to some extent, be the result of personal preference. Scarcely a town in the British Isles lacks a Gothick confection of one sort or another and the countryside is peppered with them – from great mansions to the smallest toll-house. The problem is increased by the fact that there is no such thing as a typical Gothick house, the choice and use of ornament being almost entirely arbitrary; and even the early, plain embattled houses were more abandoned in detail than their classical counterparts.

The greatest exponents of Gothick were William Kent and later, Wyatt. Their talents, combined with the amateur enthusiasm of such clients as Walpole, Beckford and many others often produced buildings of great enchantment which they believed to be in 'the true Gothic taste', but to take them too seriously today is to destroy half the enjoyment of this engaging and elusive moment in architectural history. In spite of an increased interest in medieval forms in the eighteenth century, the design and decoration of most Gothick houses was lighthearted, unrealistic and sometimes frivolous. Herein lies the magic – in these very qualities of improbability and escapism – and the further they are removed from these realms the less magical they become. This make-believe aspect is the strength and weakness of the Gothick taste.

I

Poets in
the Precincts

GOTHICK ARCHITECTURE has long been established as a style influenced, in part, by literature, linked in spirit to the poets' sentimental, romantic view of the past. Eighteenth-century writers, painters and architects looked back longingly and somewhat self-consciously to the Middle Ages, investing that period with idealised visions of pageantry, tyranny and romance. The scene was always dark and in its midst was the ancient castle, perched high on its menacing rock. The castle was Gothic, the form most suited to the melancholic mood of Romanticism and it became the Gothick architect's dream to invent his own forms of medievalism and to use them in a new context within this mood. Ruins of abbeys and monasteries, often plundered by the Elizabethans after the Dissolution of the Monasteries to build their own showy houses, became, for the first time, objects of admiration, wonder and awe. The passage of time had given them just the qualities required to stimulate the imagination and poets and painters spent endless hours under their soaring, broken vaults of Tintern and Melrose (see p. 49).

Spenser and Milton had already expressed the dramatic possibilities of the Gothic mood and Webster, ever drawn to scenes of gloom and dark deeds, shows, at the beginning of the seventeenth century, a prophetic enthusiasm for ancient buildings:

> . . . This fortification
> Grew from the ruins of an ancient abbey;
> And to yond side o' the river lies a wall,
> Piece of a cloister, which in my opinion
> Gives the best echo that you ever heard,
> so hollow and so dismal . . .[1]

It was over a century later, however, that Alexander Pope, poet and arbiter of taste in architecture and landscaping, was to publish a series of verses that showed a more distant, and therefore more romantic, feeling for ruins. This was combined with a new approach to Nature early encouraged by the Earl of Shaftesbury's *Characteristics of Men* (1711) and the web of aesthetic theories spun by a new group of connoisseurs engrossed in the idealisation of scenery and its relationship to paintings, themselves easily translated into poetic form. Pope's descriptions of the Gothic scene are artificial, dramatic and in unison with this pictorial approach to landscape; they are also some of the earliest eighteenth-century instances, and forerunners of the enormous flood of poetry and fiction devoted to the romance of buildings and their surroundings.

> . . . August and hoary, o'er the sloping dale,
> The gothic abbey rears its sculptur'd towers;
> Dull through the roofs resounds the whistling gale;
> Dark solitude among the pillars low'rs . . .[2]

wrote W. J. Mickle (1735–88) praising the joys of melancholy and gloom. Thomas Gray would continue this obsession and Wordsworth later extol the virtues of Nature herself; Turner would romanticise the ruins of Tintern, Coleridge and Blake dwell on the spiritual dilemma of man in his environment. But, partly due to the scientific relevations of Isaac Newton, Nature could be more easily understood and thus seem less terrifying and writers and painters were therefore challenged to create fresh illusions of splendour and awe. They presented all aspects of Nature as dark and dreadful menaces, essential to the Gothick mood; they frightened themselves into realms of endless gloom. Mountains would threaten overhead, clouds burst asunder, winds howl forever, each element contributing to an earthly nightmare. The turmoil of the human spirit would be set against the desolations of ancient ruins:

> I dare the dangers of the mould'ring wall,
> Nor heed the arch that totters o'er my head;
> O! quickly may the friendly ruin fall,
> Release me of my love, and strike me dead . . .[3]

wrote Chatterton in parody of the contemporary enthusiasm for disaster and decay.

But many others were more serious in the preoccupation with the delight of peril, the thought of pain and even possible death. This masochistic tendency was an important part of the aesthetic scene, Shelley referring to it as '. . . the tempestuous loveliness of terror . . .', and in our own day Mario Praz suggests that 'the discovery of Horror as a source of delight and beauty ended by reacting on mens' actual conception of beauty itself . . .'[4] Gothick tales, influenced by a revival of interest in Shakespeare, his contemporaries and newly fashionable German poetry, exploited every possibility of the Horrid; Ann Radcliffe, Mary Shelley, 'Monk' Lewis and others revelled in the cult of the strange and repellent. The background for these stories of woe was never ordered and classical, always wild and romantic:

> He approached, and perceived the Gothic remains of an abbey; it stood on a kind of rude lawn, overshadowed by high and spreading trees, which seemed coeval with the building, and diffused a romantic gloom around. The greater part of the pile appeared to be sinking into ruins, and that which had withstood the ravages of time showed the remaining features of the fabric to be more awful in decay. The lofty battlements, thickly wreathed with ivy, were half demolished, and become the residence of birds of prey . . .[5]

Few Gothick novels failed to describe the buildings in which the dark deeds would take place and the atmosphere of suspense was largely dependent on them. Byron and Keats constantly employed medieval images; George Eliot, Jane Austen and others reflect the influence of architecture on literature with their references to fashions in buildings and satirical comments upon them. It was Gray, however, who fused architecture and writing, for he had a genuine passion for Gothic buildings and, by the standards of his times, was a distinguished archaeologist. His poems, like those of the less celebrated Thomas Warton (1728–90), historian of poetry and serious archaeologist, contain all the ingredients of Gothic lore.

> Here mouldering fanes and battlements arise,
> Turrets and arches nodding to their fall,
> Unpeopled monasteries delude our eyes,
> And mimic desolation covers all.[6]

Here Gray is describing the extraordinary series of mock ruins by Lord Holland in Kent[7] and sees the basic absurdity of the idea, at the same time crystallising the eighteenth-century delight in 'fabric more awful in decay'. And it is precisely with mock ruins that we see the Gothick style emerging. Thomas Whately ends his description of Tintern Abbey by suggesting that such ruins should serve as prototypes for artificial ones:

> . . . Monkish tombstones, and the monuments of benefactors long since forgotten, appear above the greensward; the bases of the pillars which have fallen, rise out of it; and maimed effigies, and sculpture worn with age and weather, Gothic capitals, carved cornices, and various fragments, are scattered about, or lie in heaps piled up together. Other shattered pieces, though disjointed and mouldering, still occupy their original places; and a staircase much impaired, which led to a tower now no more, is suspended at a great height, uncovered and inaccessible. Nothing is perfect; but

memorials of every part still subsist; all certain, but all in decay; and suggesting at once every idea which can occur in a seat of devotion, solitude, and desolation. Upon such models fictitious ruins should be formed; and if any parts are entirely lost, they should be such as the imagination can easily supply from those which are still remaining.[8]

Sir Walter Scott was to include even more archaeology in his poetry and novels, substituting a little learning for mere sentiment.

Behind this sentimental, romantic approach to the past ran the more scholarly endeavours and researches of the antiquaries. Unlike the pioneering efforts of seventeenth-century figures such as Sir Henry Wotton who wrote *Elements of Architecture* in 1624, Sir William Dugdale and John Aubrey, the eighteenth-century antiquaries were sometimes practising architects. Their predecessors' work had led to the re-founding of the Society of Antiquaries in 1707, to be re-constituted in 1717, the year when we see the first stirrings of the Gothick spirit in Sir John Vanbrugh's castle at Greenwich. From this date the first half of the century produced men, professional or enthusiastic amateurs, who turned an earlier interest into a real passion for buildings of the past. No man of education lacked some knowledge of ancient architecture, however slight,[9] and from a long list of antiquaries who balanced fashionable sentiment with serious study a number may be singled out here.

At the end of the seventeenth century Browne Willis was born (1682–1760) and took an active part in reorganising the Society of Antiquaries and, by visiting every cathedral in England and Wales except Carlisle, acquired his great knowledge of Gothic. This he subsequently used when supplying information for rebuilding various churches including the chapel at Fenny Stratford (from 1724) and the *History of Gothic and Saxon Architecture in England* (1798) was compiled from his and the Rev James Bentham's manuscripts.

Bentham himself (1708–94) was a very remarkable man, combining his church duties (he was Rector of Feltwell St Nicholas, Norfolk) with antiquarian pursuits. His *History of the Conventual Church of Ely, from the Foundation of the Monastery*, AD *673–1771* (1771) was produced with the help of Gray whose love of Gothic was profound and influenced several antiquaries of the time including Norton Nichols (1742–1804) his close friend from 1764.

Earlier William Stukeley (1687–1765), basically a botanist and close friend of Sir Isaac Newton, had become a diligent antiquarian and from his extensive travels and researches resulted, among many publications, *Itinerarium Curiousum* (1724), *Palaeographia Sacra* (1736) and *Stonehenge* (1740).

William Cole (1714–82), although producing no books of his own, was a Cambridge antiquary who greatly assisted others and in 1765 made a protracted tour of France with Walpole. His impressive collection of manuscripts in his own hand are in the British Museum.

But James Essex (1722–84) is the most important antiquarian name of all in relation to Gothick and became one of the few professional antiquary-architects to whom the style seemed a natural outlet for his considerable talents. The son of a well-known Cambridge builder, he came under the spell of King's College Chapel early in life. He studied under Sir James Burrough and apart from his many works at Cambridge he became 'the first practising architect to take an antiquarian interest in medieval architecture'.[10] He worked extensively at Ely and Lincoln and was the friend of several antiquaries of distinction including Walpole for whom he was later to contribute the most authentic, scholarly additions to Strawberry Hill. For a long time he worked on a 'History of Gothic Architecture' which was never published, illustrations and the manuscript of which were left to the British Museum by Thomas Kerrich (1748–1828) Librarian of the University of Cambridge, himself a Fellow of the Society of Antiquaries and a draughtsman of great skill.

Another antiquary of importance was Captain Francis Grose (1731–91) whose *Antiquities of England and Wales* (published in several volumes from 1773) became a standard work [1].* He also published the *Antiquities of Scotland* (1798–91) and met Burns when on tour in search of material. His researches in Ireland were cut short by his death there.

Richard Gough (1735–1809) was elected a Fellow of the Society of Antiquaries in 1767 and became its Director 1771–97. A regular contributor from 1767 to *The Gentleman's Magazine*, he was an inveterate topographical traveller in Britain, touring the north of England and Scotland with Michael Tyson (1740–80) another antiquary and artist, and making good sketches and gathering notes for Camden's *Britannia*.

John Carter (1748–1817) was a professional architect, and a remarkably violent voice (again in *The Gentleman's Magazine* from 1798 to 1817) against unarchaeological Gothick and the reckless restoration of cathedrals. He became, in fact, the bridge between Gothick and the Gothic Revival, joining Britton and Pugin in the birth of new archaeological ideals. An ardent antiquary, he became a Fellow of the Society in 1795 and was patronised by Gough who used his drawings in his *Sepulchral Monuments* (1786–96) and other published works. Although Eastlake criticised Gough's method of drawing detail, he found Carter's draughtsmanship more to his liking and considered his *Specimens of Ancient Sculpture and Painting* (1786), dedicated to Walpole, 'a most valuable contribution to the art literature of his time'.[11] Between 1786 and 1793 Carter produced *Views of Ancient Buildings in England* in six volumes and republished in four volumes in 1824 as *Specimens of Gothic Architecture, and Ancient Buildings in England* . . . His output of drawings of abbeys for the Society was prodigious, as was his work for *The Gentleman's Magazine* and other publications and he earned the praise of Pugin for his zeal in stemming the tide of drastic cathedral restoration. His output in architecture was small, but his single-mindedness for archaeological truth was outstanding.

One of Carter's most successful works was the chapel at Winchester (1792) built by the efforts of Dr John Milner (1752 1826), Bishop of Castabala and vicar-apostolic of Western England, the stern critic of James Wyatt's cathedral restorations. Milner made the designs for the chapel himself and Carter carried them out. Milner was elected a Fellow of the Society in 1790 and became a distinguished archaeologist, his main publication being his *History, Civil and Ecclesiastical, and Survey of the Antiquities of Winchester* (1798–1801). In this volume Milner disagrees with Wren's opinion as to the origin of Gothic, calling Gothic 'pointed' and suggesting that such a shape was arrived at by the intersection of two round arches.[12] His theory started an endless flow of correspondence, much of it published, from professional and amateur alike, devoted to sometimes wild theories as to the origin of the pointed arch. And Gothic more than any other style provided the most enjoyable form of controversy for many years to come.

On the periphery of this circle of learned antiquaries mention should be made of the cleric-poet William Mason (1725–97). A friend of Gray, with a taste for antiquarian matters, he was much in tune with the mid eighteenth-century fashion for disguising banal buildings as romantic features in the landscape. In his *English Garden* (1771–81), he suggests that landscape gardeners should 'let every structure needful for a farm arise in castle semblance'. These words herald a great rash of utilitarian buildings masquerading as indigenous features in the grounds of country estates, well demonstrated at Sledmere, Yorkshire, where a farmhouse is disguised as a 'Tudor' gatehouse, probably designed by Capability Brown or Carr of York[13] [70]

---

* Numbers shown throughout in square brackets indicate monochrome illustrations: those in colour are referred to by page number.

THE
Antiquities
OF
ENGLAND
AND
Wales

By FRANCIS GROSE, Esq. F.A.S.

VOL. I. New Edition.

—I doe love these ancient ruynes:
We never tread upon them but we set
Our foote upon some Reverend History:
And questionless here in this open Court

(Which now lies naked to the injuries
Of stormy weather) some men lye enterred.
Loved the Church so well, & gave so largely to't

They thought it should have canopide their bones
Till Domsday: but all things have their end;
Churches & Cities (which have diseases like to men)
Must have like Death that we have.

Webster's Dutchess of Malfy.

London Printed for HOOPER & WIGSTEAD, Nº 212, High-Holborn, facing
Southampton Street, Bloomsbury-Square.

1 Title page from Grose's *Antiquities* . . . published from 1773. The quotation under the vignette from Webster's *Duchess of Malfi* emphasises the eighteenth-century preoccupation with buildings of the past:

'. . . I do love these ancient ruynes; We never tread upon them but we set Our foot upon some Reverend History . . .'

and later by others such as John Plaw who offers a 'Design for a Farm Yard' with a building in almshouse-Gothick style.[14]

These antiquaries and others were concerned with the history of architecture and the pursuit of archaeology; they were not always patrons of the arts but sometimes landed gentry and men of leisure, enlightened dilettanti, who, benefiting from their researches, became amateur antiquaries with a knowledge of archaeology and medieval building essential to a gentleman of taste. If he was a Goth, he would be more likely to invent his own form of Gothickery than to go very deeply into the history of Gothic and its construction. He wanted an acceptable approximation. The serious antiquaries, conversely, took more interest in the history of the pointed arch and thrived on controversy. Most architects and serious antiquaries had their own ideas about the origins of Gothic buildings: Wren thought they came from the Saracens via the Crusades, Warton from the Moors and Stukeley from the Saracens (and Druids). Perhaps Essex was nearer the truth in considering that the pointed arch had always been dictated by the use of vaulting. In 1817 Thomas Rickman was to analyse and categorise the origins of the various styles.

Here we are concerned with the style in its eighteenth-century guise but must also consider briefly whether it is a survival of earlier Gothic forms or a revival after a complete break of interest in such matters.

Eastlake clearly saw Gothick as an early, very weak phase in the Gothic Revival: 'If in the history of British art there is one period more distinguished than another for its neglect of Gothic, it was certainly the middle of the eighteenth-century.'[15] He was quite unable to appreciate a free, imaginative adaptation of an earlier style and one wonders why the eighteenth-century gothicists were more severely criticised than the classicists who plundered and adapted Palladio and Piranesi for their own purposes in much the same way. The reason was that there were strict rules for the use of the latter and none for Gothic, especially when used in an arbitrary and haphazard manner. It led to inventiveness and originality. Eastlake's distaste was based on the fact that Gothic was a structural style – a fact continually stressed in the Gothic Revival – and he therefore could not see the merits of plaster vaulting used simply to please the eye; he was unable to enjoy a little exotic fantasy for its own sake.

Lord Clark recognised that Gothic survived from the Middle Ages though tenuously, in the form of archaeology, writing and that 'tiny brackish stream'[16] of neo-gothicists whose work preceded Gothick. He also saw the frivolity of Gothick – the pretty, provocative, evocative, toy version of the thing – as a necessary stepping-stone in the history of taste towards a more serious study of a basic style. Dr Crook traces the beginning of the Gothic Revival to the posthumously Gothic houses of the late Elizabethan and Jacobean periods, when many great houses revived medieval features for purely decorative purposes; and buildings of the first half of the seventeenth-century contained elements of survival, revival and Renaissance sources.

Traditional stonemasons' ecclesiastical Gothic survived well into the mid eighteenth century and Mr Howard Colvin has described how this survival was, in 1734, to show tinges of Rococo Gothick as in the vaulted plaster ceiling of St Swithin, Worcester, by the Woodward brothers, stonemasons of Chipping Campden. Thus survival meets revival and twenty years later Rococo Gothick was in full swing at Edward Woodward's church at Preston-on-Stour, 'the only one of its kind known to have been designed by a mason with a traditional background . . .'[17] Other buildings, ecclesiastical or secular, had been since the early 1730s in the hands of architects, antiquarians, and amateurs; they had earlier turned stone into plaster, the reviled medium of mere decoration. And, with perhaps the exception of James Wyatt (whose knowledge of Gothic was to become exceptional), the very names of eighteenth-century gothicists – William Kent (1685–1748),

Robert Adam (1728–92) and John Nash (1752–1835), to mention but three professional exponents, declare it to be essentially a decorator's style and their work, however attractive, usually reflected the light-hearted and flimsy qualities true to the spirit of Rococo. Their interior decoration was not robust, nor did their buildings purvey the evil gloom so much the preoccupation of literature. Most were far removed from Peacock's 'venerable family-mansion in a highly picturesque state of semi-dilapidation . . .'[18] By moonlight a newly pinnacled tower against a sinister sky might induce a certain melancholy but, on the whole, the poets outdid the architects in their obsession with 'awful' scenes.

In architecture the darker aspects of Gothick were mostly reserved for follies, ruins, grottoes and the shadier side of landscape gardening; a broken arch, fallen masonry, dead trees, owls and ivy were little to do with the house itself but essential to the atmosphere and appearance of a hermit's retreat. Only two prominent gothicists, Walpole and Beckford, attempted to capture something of the dark, neurotic and elaborate fantasies of their own novels within their own walls.

As we have noted, Gothick was evolved partly as a survival of insular heritage and emerged at a time when the strict, alien Palladianism of the Whigs, and of Lord Burlington in particular, was at its height. Palladianism was, however, soon to be invaded by more exotic overtones – Continental Rococo, Chinoiserie and Rococo Gothick, the latter becoming most easily established from the outset owing to its familiar, indigenous qualities. It was also of course a refreshing change from the rigid orders of classicism that had held sway for so long. And the instigator of this change was none other than Burlington's own brilliant protégé, William Kent, whose virtuosity as a painter, decorator and architect in the classical mould was unique in the eighteenth century. But the change was, as with all early Gothick, only in detail; classical carcasses were given pointed windows, battlements and crocketed finials all arranged quite formally and the interiors might be classical in detail throughout. The result was simply the classical use of medieval trimmings and by the middle of the century this conventional application of ornament had spread so rapidly that it was the subject of derision and in 1756 the sharp observer of the social scene, John Shebbeare, (1708–88) deplored the rash of Gothick and Chinoiserie that appeared in all forms of furniture and in decoration. The fashion for Oriental wallpapers depicting figures 'which resemble nothing in God's creation' particularly upset him and he considered that 'a prudent nation would prohibit [them] for the sake of pregnant women'.

Scores of houses were run up with pointed windows, a vaguely Gothic porch, an odd quatrefoil opening, a pinnacle or two and a fretted parapet. These embellishments, mostly culled from an ever-increasing supply of builders' pattern books, were now the property of builders for the rising middle class, property that prompted Lord Chesterfield to coin the phrase 'Carpenter's Gothic'. As Lord Clark put it 'They built Gothic as a parvenu buys family portraits – to suggest that their pedigree stretched to remote antiquity.'[19] Something had to be done to rescue the style from ridicule and social disgrace; but we must leave this innocent, frivolous phase for a while and retreat to the solemn grandeur of the neo-Gothic that preceded it.

II

Rococo
at Random

THAT BRILLIANT TRIO OF GIANTS, Sir Christopher Wren (1632–1723), Sir John Vanbrugh (1664–1726) and Nicholas Hawksmoor (1661–1736), in spite of the splendour of their Baroque works, used a neo-Gothic or 'medieval' style during the last few years of the seventeenth and the first few years of the eighteenth centuries. Their buildings were mainly ecclesiastical or collegiate where the traditional idiom had always been Gothic, but Wren and his followers evolved a style which, whilst employing Gothic elements, was entirely Baroque in character and classical in conception. Wren's bold addition to Tom Tower at Christ Church, Oxford (1681–2) bows coldly to the past, showing little trace of an emotional attachment to the medieval – the work of an unsentimental, unwilling goth. 'His approach', notes Sir John Summerson, 'was objective and analytical . . . he selected a certain number of Gothic elements and then argued them into a whole conformable to his own classical taste.'[1] In almost direct contrast the eighteenth century was to squeeze every drop of sentiment out of its feeling for the past; boldness would be replaced visually by a frail pastiche and analysis by nostalgia. Wren's (or possibly William Dickinson's) curious neo-Tudor tower of St Mary, Aldermary (1702–4) [2], with its four elongated pinnacles linked by a quatrefoil-pierced parapet, shows an almost grudging reference to the sixteenth century. Several of the London City churches, such as Wren's St Dunstan-in-the-East of 1698 [3], have neo-Gothic steeples all of which have little to do with the traditional use of medieval details surviving in the seventeenth century.

Boldness was also the keynote to the grand, sombre compositions of Vanbrugh, but this was allied to a great enthusiasm for all things medieval and although he used little authentic Gothic detail, his work conjures up the scale and power of an heroic age. He combined romance with formality. His silhouettes are more in the spirit of Bess of Hardwick than Inigo Jones; his monumental massings are more to do with medievalism than classicism. His two mighty Baroque palaces of Castle Howard and Blenheim, together with their mock fortifications [4] and outbuildings, spread themselves over the landscape and provide a scene entirely divorced from the formal unbending Palladianism of Jones, or, later, Burlington. Vanbrugh had that extra spark of imagination that set him apart from Hawksmoor, introducing a new, forward-looking approach to free grouping combined with a passion for its origins. He was anticipating asymmetry of composition and relating buildings to their surroundings in order to achieve a picturesque scene, the basis of the Picturesque Theory of the late eighteenth century. This was, as Dr Watkin suggests, in part more in the nature of a re-instatement of Vanbrugh's own concern with picturesque theories and their associational values: 'The massing and irregular disposition, the jumping skyline, the rich uneven play of light and shade, architecture as an incident in dramatic landscape to which it is, ultimately, subordinate.'[2]

This romantic visual approach to landscape and buildings was to become an increasingly important element in the progress of the Gothick style until, finally, the principle was applied even to the irregular, fragmented arrangement of classical compositions, as, at the end of our period, we see Thomas Hope's Italianate house, The Deepdene, making up the ideally arranged picture. It was however to be over thirty years after Vanbrugh's death that anyone dared to build irregularly at the outset in either classical or Gothick taste and until then we see formal houses in medieval fancy dress.

Vanbrugh's own castle-style house at Greenwich of 1717 [5 and 6] was formal in plan and elevation (although he enlarged it asymmetrically in 1728), and it was Gothic in spirit if not in detail with its tall towers and bastion-like proportions. Set on a dramatic rise of land and in carefully considered landscaping it was, together with scattered subordinate buildings, the first mock castle complex in romantic vein and one of the earliest examples of a strong emotional feeling for the past. Vanbrugh's childhood

2 ST MARY, ALDERMARY, LONDON (1702–4) by Sir Christopher Wren and, probably, William Dickinson.

was spent in Chester, then a busy port charged with history and romance. Mr Laurence Whistler has suggested that 'his love of the picturesque and the mediaeval in architecture began in a city of towers with a river at its foot, ringed in a pink wall of Roman origin, and backed by the blue wall of Wales'.[3]

On a small scale and of about the same date is Alfred's Hall, a precocious and isolated example of the 'ruined' castle-folly. It was built by the long-lived first Earl Bathurst with the help of his close friend Pope as one of the embellishments to the magnificent landscaping of Cirencester Park.[4] It is a minor building originally containing only one room but also a masterpiece of the 'amorphous squalor of mediaevalism' as Miss Barbara Jones puts it.[5] It offers more of the 'awful' element so essential to the poets than perhaps any Gothick structure of the century. Set in a clearing, surrounded by sinister trees and shrouded with creepers, this decaying piece of deception makes most follies of later years seem the shams they are and probably contains the first pointed opening to be used in a secular building in our period.

Wren used the pointed opening in his work whereas Vanbrugh did not, the latter suggesting medievalism by composition and disposition of parts and it was left for the third member of the trio, Hawksmoor, to introduce a more fanciful note to neo-Gothic. It was some fifteen years before Kent's first Gothick efforts that he commenced the north quadrangle of All Souls', Oxford (see p. 50). He was Wren's pupil, assistant and ardent admirer and could never compete with his master's brilliance; neither could he produce a Castle Howard or a Blenheim Palace (although he worked at both) and remained somewhat of a 'back-room boy'.[6] But he was a remarkably inventive artist in his own right and his highly original and often astonishing church steeples alone give him a high place in architectural history. At All Souls' (from 1715) we can detect the lightweight character of Gothick

3   ST DUNSTAN-IN-THE-EAST, LONDON (1698) by Wren.

4 CASTLE HOWARD, YORKSHIRE: Sir John Vanbrugh's picturesque mock fortifications (from 1699).

emerging, so despised by Stukeley – the purely decorative crocketed finials and non-functional buttresses, the battlements, pendant cornices and other details later to be transferred to secular building by those with even less real interest in medieval precedents. Hawksmoor had the supreme knack of being able, especially in his City churches, to give an illusion of medievalism and the appeal of All Souls' lies not only in its fantastic Baroque towers but also in the improbability and theatricality of the whole set-piece. It is these qualities that bring it closer to the Rococo Gothick of the future.

Another bright star of this period was James Gibbs (1682–1754), again a follower and admirer of Wren, but not a pupil. He was the exact contemporary of Hawksmoor, and his reputation was established by his St Mary-le-Strand (1714–17), one of the Church Commissioners' proposed fifty new City churches. An early training in Italy had given his work a Baroque

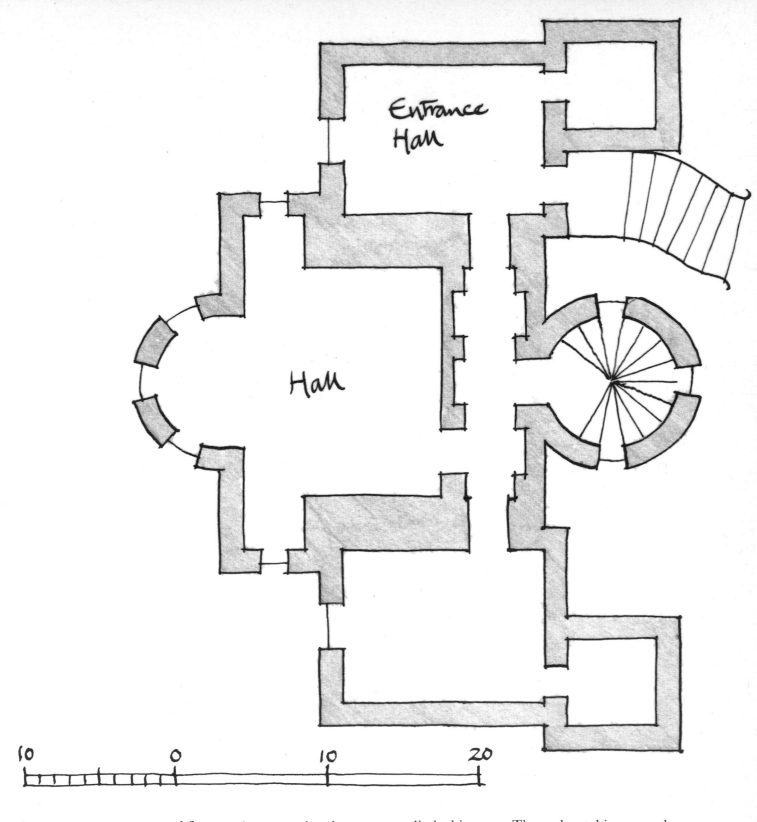

Entrance Hall

Hall

10   0   10   20

6 VANBRUGH CASTLE: ground floor plan.

5 VANBRUGH CASTLE, GREENWICH (1717), by Vanbrugh, who later added the wing to the right and made other alterations disguising the original formal plan.

character that became peculiarly his own. Throughout his career he was basically a classicist with a marked individual style and one rare excursion into Gothick, the temple at Stowe [7], also shows an equally individual treatment of the style. It is a perfect work of art in itself, a tiny asymmetrical Gothick palace in ochre-coloured ironstone, started in 1741 for the first Viscount Cobham as part of his 'political garden' where he built several temples testifying to his various political and patriotic loyalties.[7] Gibbs obviously appreciated the serious intent of his client and this sets this remarkable little building apart from the run-of-the-mill temples, follies and other landscape decorations.

Also in 1741 Kent was busy providing a Gothick choir-screen for Gloucester Cathedral [8] and, with few reservations, this amazingly versatile artist must be considered the father of Rococo Gothick. He was the first to embellish

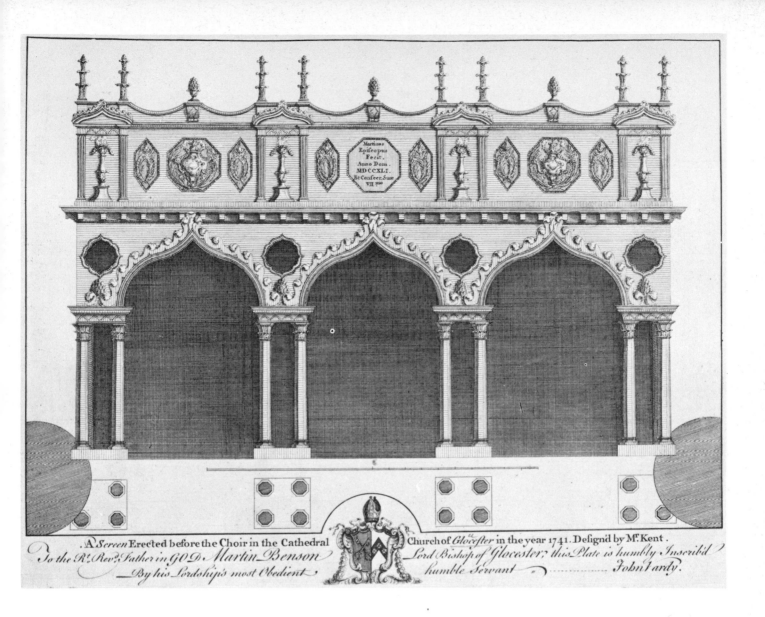

Church of *Glocester* in the year 1741. Defign'd by Mr. Kent.
Lord Bifhop of Glocefter; this Plate is humbly Infcrib'd
humble Servant . . . . John Tardy.

.A *Screen* Erected before the Choir in the Cathedral
To the Rt. Revd. Father in GOD Martin Benson
__By his Lordfhip's moft Obedient__

8 GLOUCESTER CATHEDRAL: the
choir screen (1741) by William Kent,
showing his classical disposition of
Gothic ornament.

an important domestic building with medieval detail. Eastlake makes no
mention of him and even though his output of Gothick was small, his influence was enormous. His few exercises in the idiom, completely unscholarly,
were enough to convince a host of builders and craftsmen that here was an
easily produced style combining novelty with enough authenticity to interest
a growing middle class in its medieval heritage. And as soon as it became
popular the pedants, aristocracy and leaders of fashion revolted against its
accessibility to their intellectual and social inferiors, turning to further
novelty in the form of Oriental and other exotic stimulants or, later, to what
they thought to be a more serious form of medievalism.

The craze for unscholarly medieval trimmings which Kent started was
exactly in accord with his painter-decorator-architect versatility and he
used Gothic detail as most architects would use classical. His work at
Gloucester Cathedral and at Hampton Court testifies to an unemotional
only vaguely associational appreciation of the past and he built up an almost
mechanical vocabulary of useful motifs fitting them into his ecclesiastical and
secular works. He borrowed, say, a quatrefoil and repeated it to make a
cornice or frieze just as he and others did with an acanthus leaf, dentil or
other classical motifs. Sometimes he mixed the two idioms, leaving the field
even wider open for less skilful manipulators to spread their charming, naïve
but too-popular wares. 'The Gothic of Kent, and of Batty Langley, was,
fundamentally, a free variation of classical forms constituting not an imitation but an *equivalent* of Gothic' is how Sir John Summerson describes these
early attempts at secular Gothick.[8]

7 THE GOTHICK TEMPLE, STOWE,
BUCKINGHAMSHIRE (from 1741) by
James Gibbs, who rarely departed
from the classical.

31

For thirty years, however, Kent was the most influential and celebrated architect of his day and much of his success was due to the patronage of Lord Burlington who virtually 'took him over' and employed and housed him until his death. As a painter his frescoes were attractive but poorly executed (and greatly inferior to those of his rival, Sir James Thornhill), and his decoration and furniture design showed great originality and skill. He 'lacked depth but abounded in fertile imagination' says Mr Lees-Milne.[9] And imagination, rather than truth or scholarship, was precisely the requisite of any eighteenth-century goth. But Kent's talents did not end here; his illustrations for Spenser's *The Faerie Queen* (1751)[10] reveal his imaginative use of architectural scenes, and his extraordinary grasp of the principles of landscape gardening place him as the influential predecessor to Capability Brown and the whole future of the appearance of the English country-side.

He worked at Stowe and although the full extent of his work there is not known, Miss Dorothy Stroud has pointed out that 'Kent and Brown were brought into the closest contact at Stowe, and . . . the latter's subsequent work bears the unmistakable mark of Kent's influence'.[11] And with reference to Kent's precociousness in picturesque perception, Walpole made his celebrated observation that he 'leaped the fence, and saw that all Nature was a Garden'.[12] At Rousham, Oxfordshire, between 1738 and 1741, he not only added Gothick wings to the house and remodelled part of the interior in Gothick taste, [13] but also planted and landscaped the splendid park, creating great vistas, designing Venus's Vale with its two sparkling cascades and providing many other ornamental features, freeing the country house at last from the formal surroundings of previous generations.[14] What was lost (now sadly only to be seen in views mainly by Knyff and Kip) in the form of water gardens and the meticulous patterns of box edging and magnificent formal parterres, was gained in the grand artificial sweep of the Kentian bid to create the painter's earthly Paradise.[15] Today we regret that Kent, Brown and Repton did not retain some of these wonders of garden design which were, after all, extensions of the houses themselves and could have given many opportunities for contrast between formal planning and Nature beyond. But they were swept aside and all Nature was indeed to become a garden as long as it was trained and tamed to make a picture. And the landscape conceits of Kent and others, decorating the picture all over the country, often in Gothick guise, would last for over one hundred years to be finally banished only by the Gothic Revival when, as Lord Clark notes, 'Britton killed ruins and Rococo'.[16] And, in between, Walpole was to stifle them.

For fifteen years – from Hawksmoor's All Souls' to Kent's Esher Place – Gothick seemed to be storing up its energy for the uncontrollable flood of the mid 1730s. There is nothing to suggest a link between the two (their use of medieval detail was quite differently motivated) but Kent would try his hand at anything and we might also assume that his interest in Gothic decoration was stimulated when he was commissioned to rebuild the east side of Clock Court at Hampton Court Palace in 1732. Here he was persuaded to employ a Tudor style to harmonise with the existing buildings although he had suggested a classical composition. The red brick gatehouse is one of the earliest known examples of secular Gothick and contains curious features of fenestration and decoration that proclaim it to be unauthentic. By this date Kent had already dabbled in the Tudor style, embellishing a red brick gatehouse of the late fifteenth century with even more outlandish detail a few miles away at Esher [9]. The gatehouse had been part of the palace of the Bishops of Winchester to which Kent added flanking wings to make a sizeable country house for Henry Pelham, the financier. He joined the two semi-octagonal towers with a strange porch topped by brattishing, and turned the carriageway between into an entrance hall. New ogee windows were inserted and repeated in the embattled, bay-windowed wings.

East Front of Esher place in Surry the Seat of the Right Honble Henry Pelham

9 ESHER PLACE, SURREY (c1730): a Tudor brick gatehouse remodelled by Kent.

The fourth storey of the towers were given outsize quatrefoil openings. Inside Kent added plasterwork to the brick vaulting and decorative cornices in a mixture of Greek, Gothic and floral designs.[17]

Walpole obviously relished this hybrid of history and fantasy for he exclaimed: 'Esher I like the best of all Villas, Kent is Kentissime there!'

In spite of Kent's small Gothick output it was sufficient to set a wildfire fashion which, as we have noted, became too popular (and therefore unfashionable) in carefree form. The idiom got out of hand and was used indiscriminately throughout the country. But in all its phases it enjoyed three distinct advantages: it conjured up something ancient and yet familiar; its character was in tune with the literary taste of the times; and it pandered to the snobbery of the parvenus, providing them with an illusion of long lineage. Walpole, a dedicated genealogist and proud of his family's important, but relatively recent, position in society, filled his pointed windows with arms in stained glass to produce 'the gloomth of abbeys' a notion that would have been even more absurd in a classical setting.

The desire to create a medieval ambience was attractive to the newly landed gentry, some of whom returned from the East with great fortunes and were not at all averse to giving financial support to prevailing party funds in return for a title which, in turn, demanded arms with which to decorate the new 'ancestral' home. Thus we see Gothick establishing itself as an architectural style closely influenced by the literary, sociological and political trends of the period. Alas for posterity a sickly stream of neo-Tudor persists to this day, complete with stained glass depicting not arms but the galleon in the setting sun.

It is not possible, however, to separate completely at any stage the Gothick and classical forms of the eighteenth and early nineteenth centuries; both are evocations of the past and, apparent extremes, interdependent and often interchangeable. Both are manifestations of the Romantic Movement and many neo-classicists, including Adam and Flaxman, worked in Gothick. They translated, with varying degrees of success, medieval detail into terms acceptable for their purposes. But we can still trace the progress of Gothick however much it is only a part of various architectural syntheses throughout its long course. It ends with the bright little plaster villas dotted about the countryside and more often by the sea. They are children of the Picturesque but, with their innocent lack of scholarship, take us back to the frills of Kent and show that the Rococo element was never eclipsed by the more serious students of medievalism during the second half of the century.

Several books dealing with archaeological and architectural aspects of ancient classical forms had been appearing since Sir Henry Wotton's *Elements of Architecture* and a century later, as we have seen, the learned antiquaries produced many more. The earlier archaeological volumes also dealt in certain depth with Gothic forms but by this time the Wren school was firmly established and classicism was, of course, the main topic, becoming increasingly so as Burlington's Palladianism succeeded it. So, by the time Kent was designing his choir-screen at Gloucester from his mechanical vocabulary of medieval motifs, it had become the turn of Gothick to be nailed down to rules. The outcome was Batty Langley's *Gothic Architecture Restored and Improved . . .* (1742).[18] This work had precisely the opposite effect to that intended; instead of controlling design and decoration it provided builders and craftsmen with a host of attractive details to copy, well or badly, and to apply out of context whenever a client required a touch of medievalism. Langley's optimistic but poorly written introductory essay was, in fact, a serious and honest attempt to persuade those practising the idiom that it could be disciplined and used 'correctly' for any building – from a garden pavilion to the façade of a whole house. He clearly loved Gothic and thought that there must be basic rules for its proper interpretation. His many books, published from the early 1720s, reveal his involvement with such wide-ranging subjects as landscape gardening, carpentry, gates, temples, grottoes, cascades and houses, all of which he not only designed but was also

10 HAMPDEN HOUSE, BUCKINGHAM-SHIRE (1750s): The Batty Langley-style entrance front is an addition to a larger earlier house.

prepared to construct. His issues of *The Builder's Director, or Bench-Mate* (1746, 1751, 1767) further spread his designs to professional and amateur alike. Some of the results were eccentric or amusing, such as Hampden House, Buckinghamshire of the 1750s [10], few reaching the lustre found in the dazzling garden-house at Frampton, Gloucestershire of the mid 1740s (see p. 67), the charm of the little rotunda at Goldney House, Clifton (1757) [11] or the featherweight Gothick detail at the Archbishop's Palace at Bishopsthorpe. The 1765 embellishments at Croft Castle, Herefordshire[19] (see p. 68) and the earlier remodelling of the fifteenth-century Lady Chapel at St Michael's Mount, Cornwall[20] (see p.101) are two further examples of Gothick at its most successful. Stout's Hill, Gloucestershire [12 and 13] of 1743 is the parent of the garden-house at Frampton, both possibly by William Halfpenny.[21]

12 STOUT'S HILL, GLOUCESTERSHIRE (1743): Halfpenny may have used a scaled-down version of this design, probably also by him, for the garden-house at Frampton.

13 STOUT'S HILL: a stone chimney-piece combining naïve Gothick and Rococo elements.

Fig. I.

Fig. II.

Fig. III.

Fig IV.

Batty and Thomas Langley Invent and Sculp. 1741.

14 Langley's 'Five Orders'. He published several variations of enrichments for each order (from 1742).

Langley's greatest mistake was to invent five 'orders' for Gothick [14] in an attempt to give it the status of the classical style and to make sense out of the prevailing chaotic application of elements. He overlooked the fact that the only rules that could be fairly applied were those of truthful construction, the obsession of the Gothic Revivalists, and this was the last thing that interested the Georgian architects. Apart from a Gothic-looking house itself, they also wanted pretty little features with which to decorate their gardens [15, 16]. Thus, in order to sell his Gothick to the upper classes, he had to ensure that workmen possessed handbooks for its use. So Gothick remained with such wayward whims as Chinese and Hindoo to which, mercifully for the freedom and charm of English Rococo, no rules could be applied. And in the 1740s fashion flocked to Vauxhall Gardens to enjoy the bizarre combination of Gothick and Chinese in elaborate profusion. In 1759 Paul Decker added his own exotic *Gothic Architecture Decorated . . .*[22] full of beguiling whimsies and conceits [17, 18]. Then in 1852 William and John Halfpenny produced *Rural Architecture in the Gothic Taste . . .* which included the ambitious eye-catcher of illustration 19. Later Ince and Mayhew produced their handsome guide to furniture and decoration, *The Universal System of Household Furniture* (1762–3) with several plates of Gothick designs [20].

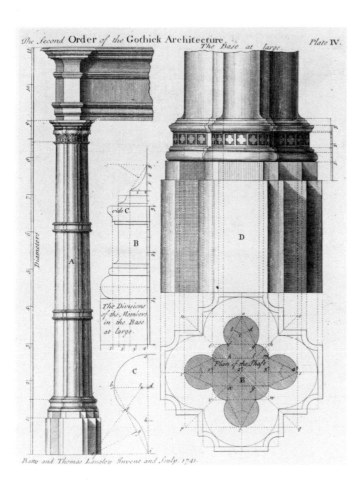

The Second Order of the Gothick Architecture.   Plate **IV**.

The Base at large.

The Divisions of the Members in the Base at large.

Plan of the Shaft

Batty and Thomas Langley Invent and Sculp. 1741.

The Fourth Order of the Gothick Architecture.   Plate **X**.

Batty and Thomas Langley Invent and Sculp. 1741.

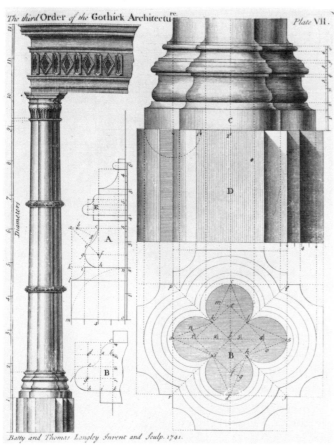

The Third Order of the Gothick Architecture.   Plate **VII**.

Batty and Thomas Langley Invent and Sculp. 1741.

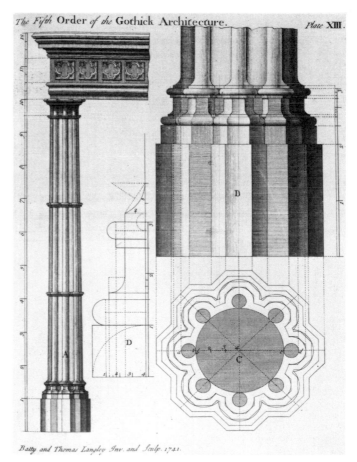

The Fifth Order of the Gothick Architecture.   Plate **XIII**.

Batty and Thomas Langley Inv. and Sculp. 1741.

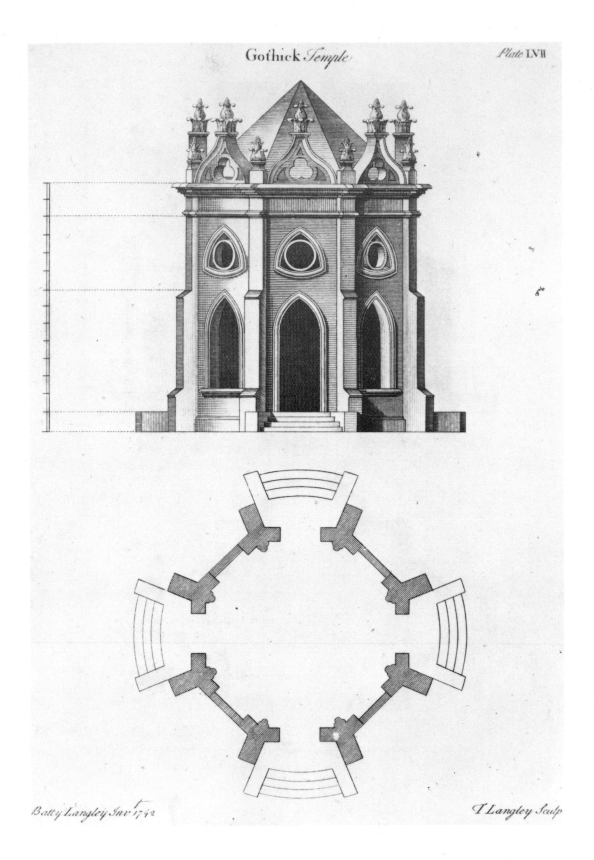

Gothick *Temple*

Plate LVII

Batty Langley Invᵗ 1742

T Langley Sculp

15 and 16   Two designs for garden temples by Langley (1742).

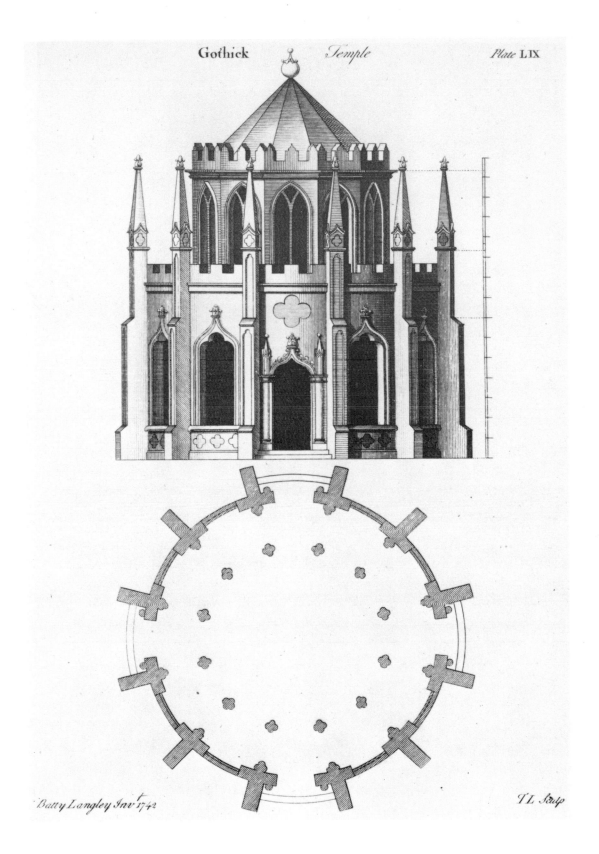

Batty Langley Inv.t 1742

TL Sculp

16

A Gothic Structure Not only Ornamental as in the figure But by different Coverings may be Easily made a Tent, Temple or Umbrellod Banqueting House &c.

17 and 18 (top and bottom) Three designs for garden buildings by Paul Decker (1759).

Rustic Garden Seat.

Alcove Seat.

Piramid of Pollard Tops

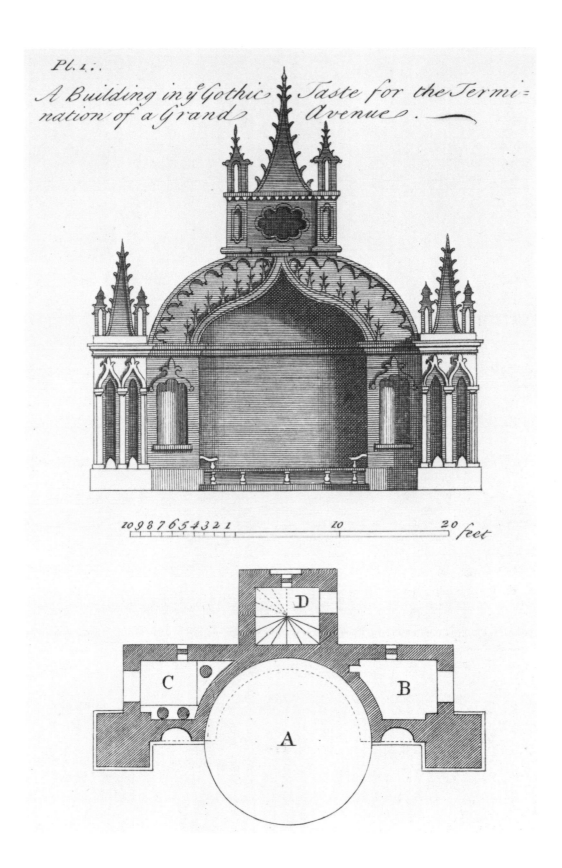

Pl. 1.

A Building in yͤ Gothic Taste for the Termination of a Grand Avenue.

20 9 8 7 6 5 4 3 2 1   10   20 feet

19   Design for a pavilion to terminate a 'Grand Avenue' by Halfpenny.

Both Langley and Walpole, for different reasons, thought they had put Gothick on solid ground and even though the latter despised the former, they both belong to the same mid-century school of Rococo. The style had

Gothic Chimney Pieces.

20 Alternative designs for chimney-pieces with 'Chinese' elements, by Ince and Mayhew (1762–3).

20 Alternative designs for chimney-pieces with 'Chinese' elements, by Ince and Mayhew (1762–3).

21 BURGHLEY HOUSE, NORTHAMP-
TONSHIRE (*c*1760): the garden-house
by Capability Brown. He also designed a Gothick greenhouse at
Burghley.

emerged from the intellectualism of neo-Gothic and was passing through the decorative, associational Kent-Langley phase towards Walpole's isolated archaeological contributions, which would later be rejected in favour of the fanatical school of structural honesty. There were many shades between but, whatever their differences, the designs of the Georgian goths remain pastiche in spite of all dissertations and researches. Archaeology had yet to win over whimsy.

Running parallel to the Kent-Langley style was what Walpole called 'Good King James's Gothic', a sort of paraphrase of Jacobean decorative motifs. At Hampton Court Kent provided ceilings in this vein for his gate-house and Vanbrugh and others had also employed plasterwork derived from seventeenth-century originals.[23] Almost anything non-classical fitted into the Gothic category. Capability Brown's garden-house at Burghley [21],

Repton's and Nash's little Tudor-Jacobean-Saxon bath-house at Corsham [22] and other hybrid garden buildings all pleased the eye of the non-classicist. The Jacobean strain was almost a tiny revival in itself but was not strong enough to compete seriously with either classical or Gothick. It would, however, return in the form of large country houses in the early nineteenth century.

Kent's work at Rousham, Oxfordshire, of the late 1730s carries us not only stylistically towards fuller Rococo Gothick but is also geographically on the borders of the Midlands where, from the early 1740s, an extraordinary group of antiquaries and amateur architects were planning some of the most exciting houses in the whole history of the style. It is in this area that we find both the most brilliant expression of secular Rococo Gothick and the transition between ecclesiastical Gothic survival and Gothick revival.

III

Mansions
of the Midlands

A GREAT TRIANGLE south-east of Birmingham, formed roughly by Kidderminster, Nuneaton and Oxford encloses the estates of several remarkable and scholarly eighteenth-century gothicists, the most outstanding being Sir George Lyttleton, James Leigh, Sir Roger Newdigate, James West, Bishop Maddox and the Earl of Guilford. All were interested in antiquarian matters and all knew and most employed the services of Sanderson Miller (1716–80), a name central to this essay and whose original handling of medieval forms radiated from the Midlands to Somerset, Cambridge, Wiltshire, Essex and even to Ireland; but the triangle remained the cradle of this 'Great Master of Gothick' and his enlightened patrons.

Miller held the affection of his clients and friends to an unusual degree and in his letters and those of his correspondents[1] we get a view of a generous, good-natured man, respected by all who knew him. With the exception of William Shenstone and Walpole, both of whom seem to have resented his popularity and success, he was highly regarded by William Pitt, Lord Dacre, Lyttleton, Newdigate and many others in the forefront of artistic and political affairs. Several were influenced by his enthusiasm for history and his letters show the pleasure he and his friends derived from their mutual interest, adding warmth and richness to their lives and making a refreshing contrast to the sour utterances of Walpole and Beckford. His self-effacing wife, Susannah, bore him seven sons and four daughters and created a rare atmosphere of generous hospitality for their wide circle of friends.

Born in 1716, the son of a prosperous Banbury wool merchant and High Sheriff of Warwickshire, Miller was a student-antiquary whilst still at Oxford where he met several of his future patrons who early appreciated his flair for architecture. He was an inspired amateur with a deep-seated passion for history and, at the age of twenty, inherited Radway Grange, Warwickshire, a modest stone Elizabethan manor house. But the house was set in the splendour of one of the county's most beautiful valleys and, as if to fire his already romantic spirit, sheltered by Edge Hill, the scene of the battle. Thus as a young man, with enough time, money and imagination, he set about the enjoyable task of embellishing his idyllic estate. In the village of Edge Hill he built a Gothick thatched cottage (1744) and then proceeded to accentuate the Gothic character of the house [23]. He added bays with pointed windows, turrets at the angles and other purely decorative elements to the Elizabethan carcass. The result was eccentric and unharmonious, but highly original. His bays, which he also patched on to Rockingham Hall, Hagley, for Admiral Thomas Smith, in 1750, were to become his trade-mark and the most easily distinguishable feature in several later houses. At Radway all glazing bars have vanished, adding to its strange appearance. At Arbury and Adlestrop [24] they remain as an essential part of new compositions in which the bays are an important part of the whole.

The battle of Edge Hill inspired Miller to build a 'ruined' castle with an octagonal tower [25] high up on the valley ridge adjacent to his thatched cottage. The 'castle' marked the spot where the King may have raised his standard and the tower was based on Guy's Tower at nearby Warwick Castle. In this commanding position the building not only commemorated history but also served as a pleasant retreat from which to view the countryside and as a spectacular eye-catcher from below. Originally the house could be approached from this spot, a drive winding its way down the steep slope of the valley. The castle has all the engaging contradictions that proclaim it to be anything but medieval – convincingly massive walls in golden Hornton stone but pierced by pretty Gothick-traceried windows of totally different weight, paper-thin battlements and, within, elegant plasterwork. Once framed by a 'ruined' arch (which has been demolished recently), the buildings were an early exercise in picturesque grouping and, for Miller, a shop-window leading to future commissions.

Behind all his activities were the indispensable services of William

23 (above) RADWAY GRANGE, WARWICKSHIRE: an Elizabethan house gothicised by Sanderson Miller from 1744. The removal of the glazing-bars has altered the character of the bay windows.

24 (right) ADLESTROP PARK, GLOUCESTERSHIRE (1759): a complete wing added to an older house by Miller employing his familiar bay windows.

ALL SOULS', OXFORD: the north quadrangle (from 1715) by Nicholas Hawksmoor.

Hitchcox who combined the disparate roles of valet and stonemason. To him and others Miller would have given instructions and sketches, and his few drawings that survive indicate that his basically amateur status was backed up by a host of talented architects and craftsmen in their various fields. He could not have been more fortunate, for in the Midlands at this time were working a number of highly skilled men, most of whom were to be concerned with Miller's buildings and those of his friends and neighbours. Robert Moor, the brillant stuccoist, worked at Radway, Arbury and that double fantasy, Alscot Park, on the banks of the Stour near Stratford-upon-Avon (see [26] and p. 102) – an imposing Gothick mansion tacked on to an earlier, prettier Gothick doll's house (1703–72) for James West who Gothicised the little church at Preston-on-Stour [27]; Henry Keene (1726–76), Surveyor to Westminster Abbey, designer of the lovely church at Hartwell, Buckinghamshire (1753-5), gothiciser of Hartlebury Castle, Worcestershire[2] (c1750) and architect of the Vandallian Tower, Uppark, Sussex (1774), worked at Arbury, Warwickshire; and the Hiorn brothers of Warwick combined with Miller on his classical Shire Hall of 1752, William's son, Francis, being the designer of the church at Tetbury, Gloucestershire. It would be difficult to imagine anyone more favourably surrounded by talent and support.

Sir George Lyttleton, squire of Hagley Hall, Worcestershire, visited Miller's tower shortly after it was completed and soon commissioned the most celebrated ruin of all for his own park [28]. It was not to lie hidden in trees – a strange object to come across suddenly – but was to stand on a prominent hill to be enjoyed from the house. Certainly it was to be backed by dark trees and covered with ivy but its most important quality was its apparent age; a battle-battered relic from an heroic age. Some of the material was taken from nearby Halesowen Abbey, perhaps a mild form of

25 EDGE HILL: Miller's mock castle built in 1745 as an eye-catcher from Radway Grange in the valley below. It anticipated many mock castles and ruins of the future. His Gothick cottage can be seen in the middle distance.

The Round House, Edge Hill
August 1862.

architectural kleptomania compared with the Elizabethan habit of plundering to build whole houses, but only one example of many where ancient ruins were depleted of their fabric to build decorative features in the landscape. The ruin was an immediate success and caused even Walpole to utter his remark, now famous in architectural annals, that it had 'the true rust of the Barons' Wars'. Lord Dacre, amateur architect and antiquary for whom Miller was gothicising a Tudor house in Essex, stated more prophetically: 'You have got everlasting fame by the Castle at Hagley, so that I hear talk of nothing else.' But Shenstone, disgruntled as ever with Miller, thought there was 'no great variety in Ye Ruin'.[3] The group is over seventy feet long with towers at each end and enclosing smaller buildings of a practical farming nature. Originally it must have been intended to use the buildings for entertaining as Miller was commissioned to design Gothick chairs for the building which were executed by Keene.

Miller, as we have noted, was also competent in the classical style and built Hagley Hall (1754–60) for Lyttleton on the lines of Houghton, Walpole's family seat in Norfolk. But it was the ruined castle that established his reputation and earned him the title of 'The Great Master of Gothick'.

Shenstone no doubt felt greatly superior to Miller in the field of landscaping and landscape buildings for by 1745 he had already designed his own series of ruins and scenes at The Leasowes and his *Unconnected Thoughts on Gardening* (1764) set out his ideas as to how follies and their surroundings should be enjoyed: 'When a building or other object has once been viewed from its *proper point,* the foot should never travel to it by the same path which the eye had travelled over before.'[4] The game was to approach the building from another angle and 'discover' it all over again at closer quarters, as so marvellously demonstrated in the landscaping at Scotney Castle, Kent. Shenstone's gardens and those of Charles Hamilton at Pain's Hill, Surrey,

26 ALSCOT PARK, GLOUCESTER-SHIRE (from 1749): the creation of James West and his builders. The engraving shows the south front containing a suite of rooms of 1762. The smaller north wing contains decorations of the prettiest early Rococo Gothick.

28 HAGLEY HALL, WORCESTER-
SHIRE: Miller's momentous sham
castle of 1749.

27 ST MARY, PRESTON-ON-STOUR,
near Alscot Park, partly remodelled by
Edward Woodward for James West
(from 1753). The nineteenth-century
stencil decorations on the barrel-
vaulted ceiling have been removed.
The sculpture by R. Westmacott has
a dark marbled background.

for which the delectable little temple [29] was designed (c1740), are examples
of the growing desire to make each view resemble a separate picture and,
almost always, a Gothick confection would play its part – to be seen, lost
and regained in the carefully contrived landscaping. Classical temples
however, would be more openly displayed or used to close vistas; Gothick
ones would often moulder in sad, secret places, shrouded by sinister trees
and undergrowth as at Cirencester, Pain's Hill and Stourhead. Miller
reversed this practice and placed his ruins in prominent positions, another
even larger one being his castle-folly at Wimpole Hall, Cambridgeshire of
1750 for Lord Hardwicke [30]. On an immense scale, the folly differed in
many ways from that at Hagley. Two stretches of ruined wall linked by a
central prospect tower are set at right-angles on a hill and the trees behind
conceal the fact that the structure is merely one wall thick. It is an eye-catcher
from the house and park as was Kent's screen at Rousham of ten years
earlier. In the Red Book at Wimpole, Humphry Repton, who later converted
the 'ruin' into a keeper's lodge, wrote that it was 'one of the best of its kind
extant'. Repton often produced hand-written, illustrated theses for his
clients which explained his plans for landscaping the grounds and sometimes
suggesting a new house or a remodelling of an existing one. Some of the
illustrations folded out to display the schemes before and after the proposed
alterations and the books were bound in red morocco.

In the same year Miller was working at Enville, Staffordshire where he
designed several attractive small landscape buildings for the Earl of Stamford.
Here again he came up against the disapproval of Shenstone who was about
to make improvements to the grounds. He described how the Earl was
'now building a Gothic green-house by Mr Miller's direction and intends
to build Castles and God-knows-What . . . '5 In fact, they form a charming
little précis of mid eighteenth-century buildings including a Langley-style

summer-house (sometimes described as the museum or billiards room) with elaborate interior plasterwork, a pretty pedimented boathouse with Gothick detail [31] and, most engaging, a tiny, round Claude-like chapel with pointed openings[6] [32].

The year 1750 also saw Miller converting the old library at All Souls', Oxford, into rooms for Robert Vansittart, Fellow of the college and friend of Hogarth and Dr Johnson. Vansittart did not like the plaster ceiling of 1598 but Miller persuaded him to keep it and included it in a scheme of Gothick wood wall panels and doors.[7] At the same time Miller was re-designing the church tower at Wroxton and the chapel window at Wroxton Abbey, Oxfordshire,[8] for the testy Francis North, Earl of Guilford and providing an open Gothick rotunda by the lake with adjustable wind-screens for which Keene supplied working drawings.

The 1750s were Miller's busiest years and the beginning of the decade sees him working for the remarkable Sir Roger Newdigate, creator of that most brilliant house, Arbury Hall. It was then that Newdigate started to gothicise his gabled Elizabethan house of c1575 – a transformation that took over fifty years. The result was a series of the most consummate Rococo Gothick rooms ever designed, the combined efforts of many artists and financed gradually from estate funds. Newdigate made the project his long and presumably most uncomfortable life, for he died at the age of eighty-seven, the house still not completely finished.

The new exterior stone casing of the old house is in formal, solid, 'Cathedral-Gothick' style [33] giving little hint of the transcendent scenes within. But the great 'Tudor' bay windows with carved panels between the stories, the cresting and towers topped by cupolas are unmistakably grander versions of the features we see at Radway and Adlestrop; the broad expanses of wall on the north and east fronts lead us to Miller's sparing distribution of features at Lacock Abbey to come.

Newdigate, Member of Parliament for Oxford, scholar and founder of the

29 PAIN'S HILL, SURREY: the Gothick temple of c1740. Walpole disapproved of the pendant tracery.

30 WIMPOLE HALL, CAMBRIDGE-SHIRE: the sham castle by Miller of 1750.

GOTHIC TOWER at WIMPLE.

31 (above) ENVILLE HALL, STAF-
FORDSHIRE: the boathouse by Miller
of 1750.

32 (above right) ENVILLE HALL:
Miller's chapel of 1750.

33 ARBURY HALL, WARWICKSHIRE
(from 1750): the south front by
Miller, Henry Keene and others. The
bay window on the right contains the
saloon.

Newdigate Verse Prize, was himself an accomplished draughtsman and enthusiast of medieval history and he gathered about him experts in their own fields very much in the same way as Walpole was about to form his Committee of Taste at Strawberry Hill. It was not unusual for an eighteenth-century proprietor to procure the services of a band of artists and craftsmen, some of whom would remain exclusively for several years on an estate. Lord Barnard and his heirs employed Thomas Wright, James Paine and finally John Carr in the spectacular Gothick re-modelling of Raby Castle, Co Durham[9] and many others formed similar groups often fighting over the services of one prominent artist or another.

At Arbury the 'committee' consisted of Miller, Keene, Henry Couchman (an architect-contractor under the patronage of Lord Aylesford at at Packington, Warwickshire), William Hiorn, leading architect and mason of Warwick and Robert Moor, the stuccoist. Keene, less prolific as a secular gothicist than Miller but no less successful in his equally brief career, supplied drawings for the interior of the house in 1762 and was the author of many ecclesiastical and collegiate works. There can be little doubt that Newdigate employed him because of his firsthand knowledge of Westminster Abbey and therefore could entrust him with the elaborate fan-vaulting and other features derived from the Abbey. In fact, no one working at Arbury, even Keene, were serious scholars of Gothick; all were talented enthusiasts, accounting for the interiors of surpassing brilliant beauty which, in more pedantic hands, would have shown more archaeological accuracy and structural honesty, less inspired fantasy. Fortunately, as yet, there was no John Britton to put matters 'right'.

Miller's hand in the building of the house is obscured by the fact that few of his drawings survive and that illness probably removed him from the scene at an early date. Among Newdigate's own drawings and plans for the house[10] are sketches for Lady Newdigate's dressing room by Miller and a few drawings for Gothick projects possibly by him exist and may be connected with Arbury.[11] It seems that he was more likely to give inspired sketches to masons and other craftsmen and rely upon experienced draughts-men like Keene to supply working drawings.

In the new rooms at Arbury not one arch, column or vault bears any relation to structure and the decorations are merely evocative derivations of medieval originals. A low, plaster-vaulted corridor links rooms of increasing splendour, the centre-piece being the lofty saloon [34] with its white fan-vaulted ceiling based on Henry VII's Chapel and executed by Couchman in the 1780s. It is a tour-de-force of magnificence, the plasterer being William Hanwell, successor at Arbury to Moor, and requires little or no wall decoration or other competition in any form. Nearly a century later George Eliot, whose father was Agent at Arbury, compared the plasterwork with 'petrified lacework' and described how the house was 'growing from ugliness into beauty' when she used it as the model for Cheverel Manor in *Mr Gilfil's Love Story*[12] and certainly there are no more radiant Rococo Gothick rooms in existence, part of their magic being due to their dedicated adherence to a theme – as harmonious as the later classical interiors of Adam or Wyatt.

The dining-room contains canopied niches containing classical statues, similar to those at Lacock and to be used on a grander scale fifty years later in Porden's Eaton Hall. This mixture of classical and 'medieval' seems entirely acceptable and in fact the contrast between the two is at once attractive and exotic. The room that breaks with the consistent elaboration of the saloon, dining-room and drawing-room (equally sumptuously decorated) is the 'Perpendicular' library [35] where only the white, wide-arched bookcases are Gothick – a foil to the shallow barrel-vaulted ceiling of classical design composed of painted medallions and gilded scroll-work.

Although the exterior of Arbury might have some claims to 'gloomth'

35   ARBURY HALL: the library.

(and certainly gravity) the interior is far removed from the literary fashion to produce an atmosphere of melancholy, for the feeling is entirely one of lightness and grace, as Rococo as could be, banishing all the shadows with which the word Gothick is associated. Arbury is more celestial than infernal.

Whatever the full extent of Miller's contribution to Arbury, we know that he was almost entirely responsible for the important additions to Lacock Abbey, Wiltshire, for John Ivory Talbot in 1754–5. Here he built a new great hall and a gateway to span the approach [36]. The interior of the hall (see p. 119) was made to appear as monastic as possible with bare stone walls in keeping with what was to remain of the existing medieval monastery, but the basically light-hearted approach of the mid eighteenth century to the past triumphs once more and swirling terra-cotta figures 'allusive to the history of the monastery' sprout from pinnacled niches.[13] Thus the 'medieval' and the Baroque are united to form a Gothick extravaganza. The shallow, barrel-vaulted ceiling is, as in the library at Arbury, classical in form but here it is decorated with quatrefoil panels into which are fitted, none too happily, the shield-shaped arms of Talbot and his local friends.

The exterior of the hall with its widely spaced features also shows Miller's originality at work; all the seductive, unmistakable elements of Rococo are there – the fretted cresting of Venetian flavour linking the 'Tudor' cupola, the central star-shaped opening between pronounced ogee windows with carved hood moulds continued as a string-course and the external staircase with crocketed pinnacles as newel posts. All these features, and more, supplemented by Langley's books, were now in the hands of less skilled artists, those without Miller's undoubted if uneven flair. The gateway, too, flanked by richly carved finials, provides another unscholarly but lively and cheerful touch to this highly theatrical set-piece. He was, in the phrase of Mr Nicholas Cooper, a 'style-setter'.[14]

36   LACOCK ABBEY, WILTSHIRE (1754–5): the gateway with the great hall beyond, Miller's additions to the existing medieval monastery.

60

POMFRET Castle, Arlington street, built by Lady Pomfret. Aº 1760.

Almost the end of his career was marked by perhaps the most astonishing creation of all, Pomfret Castle of 1760 [37] – astonishing because the castle was in Arlington Street, London. It was a glorified toy fort for the Countess of Pomfret, widow of the first Earl, and enjoyed the best of both worlds – a town mansion with a country aspect. A low gatehouse (later much enlarged) led into a private forecourt beyond which was the house backing onto uninterrupted views of the Green Park, the central features of the main block taking us back to Gibbs's temple at Stowe. Walpole, ever delighted at disaster, then at his own house at Arlington Street, described a storm in 1779 when 'one of the stone Gothic towers at Lady Pomfret's house (now Single-speech Hamilton's) in my street fell through the roof, and not a thought of it remained'. Lady Pomfret [38], whom Walpole found a great bore, escaped this catastrophe, dying a year after Miller had completed the house in 1761. The interior contained much rich 'Perpendicular' decoration and the staircase hall [39], panelled with blind tracery, was lit by a dome set in plaster fan-vaulting.[15] But the house, unique as it was, stood on ground ripe for greedy development and was demolished in 1934 to make way for a mock-Monte Carlo block of flats, totally alien to its surroundings.

We must leave Miller on another forlorn note, back in the country, where he designed his most spectacular folly – a sham castle at Prior Park, Bath,

38 (above) The Earl and Countess of Pomfret by Bardwell.

39 (right) POMFRET CASTLE: the staircase and 'perpendicular' plaster blind tracery.

37 POMFRET CASTLE, ARLINGTON STREET, LONDON (1760) by Miller. The gatehouse leading to a courtyard in front of the house with Green Park in the background.

40 PRIOR PARK, BATH: Miller's sham castle of 1762.

for Ralph Allen [40]. This is another fort, but of a different order; it is a giant's toy – a shallow, castellated fraud with embattled towers silhouetted dramatically against the skyline. Allen knew Miller through their mutual friend, William Pitt who suggested the '. . . considerable Gothick object which is to stand on the Hills near Bath'.[16] The date is 1755 but it was not built until 1762, two years after Miller had gone insane.[17] He recovered but never again worked at full pitch and his bout of insanity seems to coincide with his replacement by Keene at Arbury.

Miller, therefore, introduces us not only to a group of brilliant men and their buildings but also leads us on to a new element in Gothick – the increasing interest in archaeology. Although he was an antiquary with a romantic appreciation of historical associations and their evocation in architecture, he worked with those, like Newdigate, who were using replicas of isolated medieval detail in fantastic settings. They imagined, as did Walpole, that an isolated version of an ancient tomb to surround a fireplace, totally out of its original context, would be sufficient to lend authenticity to the whole interior. Fortunately for the future of eighteenth-century Rococo Gothick, their imaginings were as fantastic as their houses turned out to be.

IV

Twilight on the Thames

THE LIBRARY AT ARBURY has been compared with that at Strawberry Hill and although they have similarities and are coeval, the houses themselves are utterly different in conception. Arbury with its Georgian suites of rooms is formal in plan, whereas Strawberry was enlarged over the years and became asymmetrical by sporadic additions, dictated by interior requirements. But where Walpole found freedom in planning, he became trapped in another sense; the tendency to copy isolated medieval features for internal embellishment as Newdigate had done to a certain extent, became a mania with Walpole who now began to despise the use of Gothic detail without care and attention being paid to reproduction of detail. He attempted to make Gothick respectable again by more accurate copying of monuments and the use of engravings in Dugdale's *Monasticon* (from 1655), in order to give the style status and an authentic provenance. By so doing, he was one of the first to dampen the charm of Rococo although, ironically, the result at Strawberry was still pastiche; it was no nearer the real thing even with these efforts to rescue the style from the slough of its lightweight beginnings. '. . . more than anyone,' says Dr Crook, 'Walpole killed the freedom of Rococo by popularising the cult of archaeology.'[1] The magic and fantasy were vanishing under the first shadows of reality.

Walpole's immediate circle was more sophisticated and tight-knit than Miller's and Strawberry embraced the talents of three people most concerned with its evolution: Walpole himself, John Chute and Richard Bentley. Others, William Robinson (the builder and executant), Thomas Gray, with whom Walpole made the Grand Tour, Thomas Barrett, John Carter and James Essex, the antiquaries, and Robert Adam and James Wyatt made their own contributions. But all were under the basic scrutiny of Walpole's 'Committee of Taste'.[2] The committee was virtually a research team and the members spent many months discussing whether or not to include a certain adaptation of an ancient design for the embellishment of the interior of the house as it grew. They travelled far and wide, returning with ideas and sketches which would be discussed in detail, usually in gratifying harmony, sometimes with unreconcilable differences. Chute inherited The Vyne in Hampshire, a house with qualities to inspire even the most visually-deprived visitor. Chute, however, was a man of unusual imagination and, apart from making some exceptional alterations to The Vyne, he was the author of Donnington Grove, Berkshire[3] [41 and 42] and Chalfont House, Buckinghamshire, both lovely exercises in Rococo Gothick, Chalfont being described by Walpole as 'the prettiest house in the world . . .' In spite of permanently poor health (he lived on a diet of milk and turnips as a supposed antidote to gout),[4] he travelled extensively with Walpole, shared with him an enthusiasm for genealogy and together they made the Grand Tour, partly with Gray, from 1739–41. Chute became the more solid pillar of the Committee, whom Walpole considered '. . . an exquisite architect, of the finest taste, both in the Grecian and Gothic styles', Bentley later fading out of the picture under a cloud but, fortunately, not before he had provided the most fantastical of the designs for the interior of Strawberry. Bentley, son of the distinguished Master of Trinity, had a great flair for the lighter side of Gothick and was the author of the beautiful drawings for Gray's *Six Poems* (1752), elegant and graceful to the highest degree and presenting Rococo at its most alluring. No scholar, Bentley leaned more towards the waywardness of Kent than to the comparative discipline of the archaeologists. The chimneypieces and other designs for Strawberry are of whimsical invention, skilful and highly entertaining but, as Walpole was later to complain, a far cry from the new fad for accuracy.

Walpole's dedication to the building of Strawberry is bound up with his elusive, complex character. On the whole his unattractive qualities were outweighed by his good ones, particularly his loyalty to a large circle of friends and to his family. Strawberry should, in a sense, be considered a

FRAMPTON COURT, GLOUCESTERSHIRE (c1752): the garden-house, probably by William Halfpenny, with its formal canal.

member of this circle for his devotion to it never faltered. The sour-tongued
Macaulay however, found him 'the most inconstant of men' and he could
be jealous, malicious, snobbish and small-minded; lately he was described
as 'that unpleasant dilettante'.[5] But he was also extremely industrious and
his informative correspondence alone would daunt most men and makes
compulsive reading. His ubiquitousness, probably stemming from loneli-
ness, makes it difficult to consult a memoir of his times without reading
his name. Strawberry, reflecting some of his inconsistencies of character,
turned out to be a mixture of the sound and the gimcrack, the serious
and the frivolous, the authentic and the false. But, like its creator, it is
never dull.

He was, in fact, aiming for the impossible – authenticity combined with
modern comfort and his attempts at authenticity sounded the first death-
knell of Rococo. He wanted 'true rust' and 'barbarism' but not at the ex-
pense of the 'modern refinements in Luxury'. His novel *The Castle of Otranto*
(1764), describes all the desirable qualities of doom, horror, darkness, and
infernal melancholy, qualities he was prepared to reflect at Strawberry only
in the form of a little stained glass. It was all rather absurd but at times he

42 DONNINGTON GROVE: the staircase landing.

convinced himself that Strawberry was Otranto and in the novel his wildest Gothick dreams came true.

The house, like its owner, has been described many times before[6] but here we should consider the more original aspects of the building, especially its plan [51] (see p. 81), that make it such a landmark in architectural history. 1750 is a magic date in Gothick terms and sees the birth of Arbury, Alscot, Strawberry and several other houses of essentially Rococo character. It was in 1749 that Walpole wrote to his long-suffering correspondent in Italy, the diplomat Sir Horace Mann, and asked him to look out for pieces of coloured glass as he was about to transform an ordinary little house overlooking the Thames at Twickenham into a villa with all the fashionable trappings of pinnacles, castellations and pointed windows.

Walpole's passion for the medieval may be attributed partly to a reaction against his classical background, Houghton in Norfolk, built by Colen Campbell in 1721 for his father, Sir Robert Walpole, the Whig Prime Minister. It was in the mould of Burlington's Palladianism, the antithesis of Romanticism and Horace, a natural romantic, required, like most other mid eighteenth-century dreamers, a romantic house in which to live and

Over page

43 RADNOR HOUSE, near Strawberry Hill, of the early 1750s, which
contained fine classical rooms on a
small scale.

44 STRAWBERRY HILL: the library,
with bookcases of painted wood.

indulge his taste for collecting relics from the past. He considered Grecian
forms suitable only for public buildings and lacking in 'charming irregu-
larities'. Magnificent, classical Houghton simply would not do and so he
set about the task of creating his own famous fantasy at Twickenham –
modest at first but soon to become the greatest architectural curiosity of its
time.

From all accounts, the original house on the site was an uninspiring little
place but the lovely meadows in which it was set reached down to the river,
beyond which could be seen the wooded slopes of Richmond Hill. It was
chiefly for its idyllic situation that Walpole purchased the remainder of a
lease from a Mrs Chenevix, owner of a celebrated toy shop in London. He
had also placed himself in a fashionable district full of architectural, artistic
and literary attractions. Pope, who had died two years earlier, had built a
villa next door, Kneller lived nearby and the many houses on the river such
as Radnor House, another early Gothick mansion [43] were occupied by
distinguished people calculated to prove rewarding neighbours.[7] Before
embarking on the transformation of the property Walpole acquired the free-
hold and by 1753 had turned the place into a Gothick villa, the first stage in
its dramatic metamorphosis.

Walpole's devotion to his little house amounted to a consummate calf-
love, and, even during the great additions to follow, never again reached
such an emotional intensity. His correspondence is full of the excitement he
found in planning the gardens, planting trees and creating his own, private
paradise which he would live to see grow to full maturity. The centre of his
life from now until his death nearly fifty years later was to be Strawberry
Hill.

The first major addition was the staircase started in 1753 to the designs of
Bentley who was to remain as Walpole's chief designer for ten years with

William Robinson, the builder and architect, as executant. The staircase hall had all the contradictions of reality and fantasy, deception and honesty. Even Walpole's imagination must have been taxed to believe that 'venerable barbarism' could be really created from such flimsy materials as fretted wood, plaster and wallpaper. With its original decorations it certainly must have been exceedingly pretty, with its open Gothick balusters and wallpaper painted to imitate tracery lit by a lantern of yellow glass, but scarcely barbarous. In fact the decoration of the entire interior at all its stages was theatrical and entirely artificial. The Gothick bookcases in the library [44] of painted wood, were derived from the stone doors in the screen of Old St Paul's and the chimneypiece was inspired by John of Eltham's tomb. Bentley's designs for the bookcases were rejected by the Committee who decided to adapt ancient designs from engravings rather than rely on Bentley's wayward whimsicality. The result, however, was somewhat absurd despite these references to early designs, owing to the alien purpose to which they were put. The materials used – wood and plaster instead of stone – further encouraged unreality but never sufficiently to achieve the harmless flights of fancy earlier conjured up by Bentley. Many variations of fanciful Gothick bookcases were now to appear on more modest scales like those at Malmesbury House, Salisbury (1750s) [45] for James Harris, contemporary of Newdigate at Oxford, at Milton Manor, Berkshire (c1764) [46] and later at Stowe [47] by Sir John Soane in 1805.

But it is Bentley's Strawberry that wins the day and towards the end of his life, Walpole must have realised this when he wrote to Miss Berry in 1794 that his creations were 'more the works of fancy than imitation'.[8] More precisely he might have written that his imitations had been made ridiculous by the context in which he placed them. And is not a medieval tomb masquerading as a chimneypiece on nodding terms with a cocktail cabinet disguised as the Tower of London? A cowshed imitating a classical or Gothic ruin can at once enhance the landscape but, when these ideas are transferred to the intimate details of interior decorations, adaptation of ornament must be as skilful as Adam's and as imaginative as Bentley's.

With all its contradictions the 'Decorated' library was given a certain sombre dignity by Chute, making the elaborate rooms to follow seem bizarre and tawdry. For the Holbein Chamber (so called because it contained drawings of the royal Holbein portraits) Bentley made his last designs, that for the chimneypiece [48] based on Archbishop Warham's tomb in Canterbury Cathedral and an intricate screen derived from the choir gates at Rouen. Both are in his most fantastic vein in spite of their origins.

By 1761 Walpole found he could no longer endure what he considered Bentley's unforgivable shortcomings. His brilliant and original designs did not compensate for his innate laziness and extravagance and Walpole, the arch-snob, was also upset when he brought his tiresome wife to the house when people of the highest rank were present. The breach of friendship was final and from now on designs at Strawberry were to be devised by Chute until his death in 1776 and the recently co-opted Thomas Pitt, a nephew of the Great Commoner. Adam provided a ceiling and chimneypiece and decorations for the round room in 1760, and there would be later additions by Wyatt and Essex.

Until the departure of Bentley the alterations to the original building had not been on a large scale but in 1760 we see the beginning of Strawberry's most important contribution to eighteenth-century architectural history – the addition of the cloister and the gallery above it stretching westwards and terminating in a great round tower. Because he wanted extra rooms of certain shape he tacked them on to the existing ones and in the process produced the accommodation he wanted encased in an asymmetrical, romantic shell. It was to set the pattern of country house design until the present day.

The cloister, one of Chute's plainer designs, was, in effect, an open-arched

46 MILTON MANOR, BERKSHIRE: the library of 1764–5.

verandah, a feature to be used in countless houses of the future especially by Nash whose open colonnades, whether classical or Gothick, are often an indispensable part of the design. The gallery above [49] takes us again into the realm of fact, fantasy and what today could only be called *chic*. Over fifty feet in length and thirteen feet wide it was the largest room in the house and was intended to resemble a Tudor long gallery. Bentley could have woven a magic over the walls and ceiling as had been done at Arbury and would soon be done by Adam at Alnwick; but Walpole, Chute and Pitt, partly due to their attention to medieval art, partly due to lack of inspired fantasy, produced a room at once spectacular, gaudy and 'smart'. A knowledge of archaeology had not helped to evoke the Middle Ages; walls covered with crimson damask, rich and rare in itself, did not make an authentic-looking spring-board for even a false, plaster, fan-vaulted ceiling copied from

47 STOWE, BUCKINGHAMSHIRE: Sir John Soane's library of 1805–6. The chimneypiece and stove are of brass.

Chimney Piece of The Holbein Chamber.

48 (above right) STRAWBERRY HILL: the chimneypiece in the Holbein Chamber by Richard Bentley.

Over page

49 STRAWBERRY HILL: the gallery over the cloisters.

a side aisle in Henry VII's chapel. Elaborate canopied niches taken from Archbishop Bourchier's tomb were ranged along the wall opposite the windows. They were decorated with looking-glass covered with gold net-work, scarcely materials to remind us of the rugged past. The settees, chairs and stools were also covered in crimson damask and their frames were painted black and gold. A specially woven Moorfields carpet filled the centre of the floor-space, the remainder of which contained the ranks of furniture and tables laden with sculpture and other treasures. Against the crimson damask walls were hung the best of his large collection of paintings including family portraits and those of celebrities, topographical paintings and works of curiosity and oddity. The windows were filled with the quarterings of the Walpoles in painted glass which must have provided one of the few illusions of antiquity in a room so packed with the luxurious trappings of the times.

But all the new rooms, large and small, were to be crammed with this magpie's *objets* from works of art of the highest merit to trivial mementoes of friends and the famous. Upon completion the house was still called 'Mr Walpole's Villa' but, in fact, he was creating something of his own Castle of Otranto – as near as he dared without losing one touch of flamboyance, richness and comfort. It was a brilliantly coloured creation, exotic and strange but, like a butterfly, for the moment only. Walpole's interest in archaeology alone would point to the future, his manner of presenting it would then be utterly despised. Eastlake is surprisingly lenient in his judgement of Strawberry and considered that the various alterations and additions made up 'a straggling but not unpicturesque mass of Buildings'.[9] He sees, in common with most critics of the house, the error of using ancient models out of context but does not draw attention to the gaudy, tinselly qualities of the interiors that perversely dispelled any illusion of genuine antiquity and the essential bleakness that went with it. The great bedchamber was built to the north of the gallery and, adjoining it the celebrated Chapel, later called the Tribune and later still the Cabinet. The latter description is the most accurate for, in spite of its ecclesiastical air, this small room with semi-circular apses in each wall,

50 STRAWBERRY HILL, MIDDLESEX (from 1750): the north front, with Walpole's original little house on the left and later additions terminating with the large round tower.

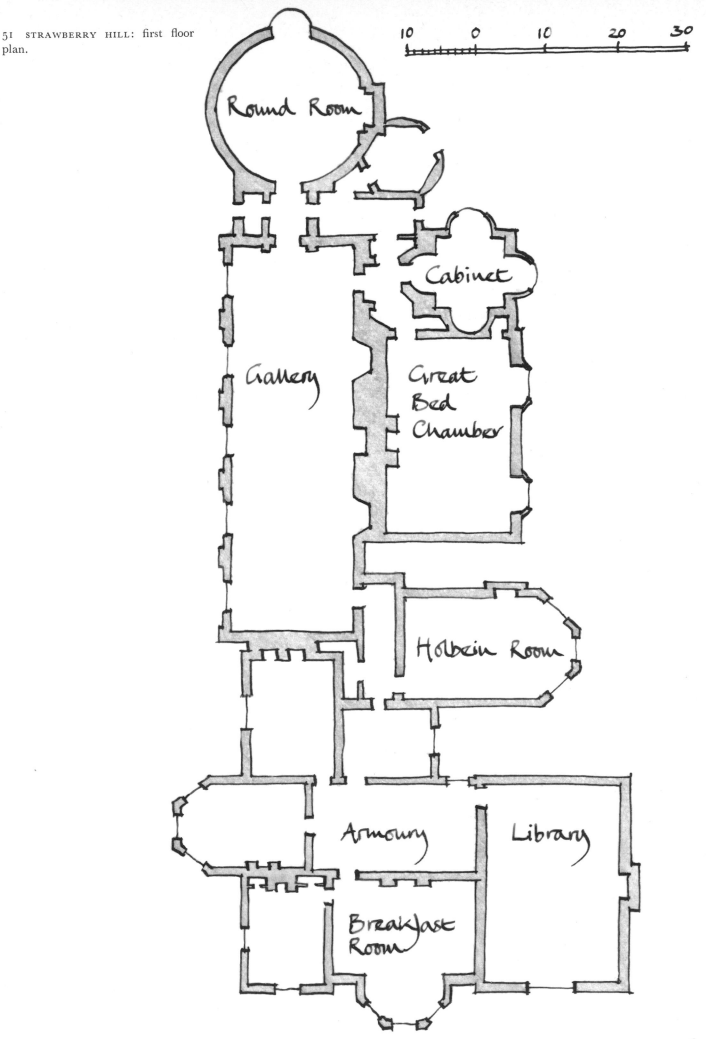

10   0   10   20   30

Round Room

Cabinet

Gallery

Great
Bed
Chamber

Holbein Room

Armoury   Library

Breakfast
Room

plaster ceiling derived from the Chapter House at York pierced by a central yellow glass star-shaped skylight, became a repository for all manner of unholy objects from statues of Antonius and the Apollo Belvedere to a snuff-box of lapis lazuli. Every available inch of wall-space was hung with portraits, few of them of religious subjects but all of family, historical or artistic interest.

With the addition of the round tower, containing the kitchen on the ground floor and the round drawing-room with great bow window on the first floor, and the slimmer attendant tower, Walpole's complex was, with the exception of later offices, complete [50]. During its building it had naturally created a considerable amount of curiosity and with mixed feelings Walpole decided to admit members of the public to see the house and its collection. A leaflet, printed on his own private press in 1784, gives somewhat daunting instructions to intending visitors:

> Lord Orford[10] is very ready to oblige any curious persons with the sight of his house and collection; but as it is situated so near London and in so populous a neighbourhood, and as he refuses a ticket to nobody that sends for one, it is but reasonable that such persons as send should comply with the Rules he has been obliged to lay down for showing it.
>
> Any Person sending a Day or two before, may have a Ticket for Four Persons for a Day certain.
>
> No Ticket will serve but on the Day for which it is given. If more than Four Persons come with a Ticket, the Housekeeper haspositive Orders to admit none of them.
>
> Every Ticket will admit the Company only between the Hours of Twelve and Three before Dinner, and only One Company will be admitted on the same Day.
>
> The House will never be shown after Dinner; not at all but from the First of May to the First of October.
>
> As Lord Orford has given Offence by sometimes enlarging the Number of Four, and refusing that Latitude to others, he flatters himself that for the future nobody will take it ill that he strictly confines the Number; as whoever desires to break his Rule, does in effect expect him to disoblige others, which is what nobody has a right to desire of him . . .
>
> They who have Tickets are desired not to bring Children.

Thus Strawberry became the showplace of its age and few of the people who flocked to see it would realise the significance of Walpole's rambling fantasy. He had succeeded in producing the first irregular, picturesque house since Vanbrugh at Greenwich. Vanbrugh's was accidental but it is difficult to believe that Walpole's irregularity was not, in part, deliberate. At no time does he apologise for it and there is no doubt that he was fully conscious of the final silhouette that his buildings would make. He is known also to have appreciated 'Sharawaggi or Chinese want of symmetry in buildings as in grounds or gardens'. It is customary to think of Strawberry becoming irregular by accident but at least its creator knew that it was a happy accident. His little crocketed house joined by a gallery and ending in a round tower takes us far away from formal planning towards the ideals of the Picturesque – ideals that were to place more importance on the total pictorial effect of a building in relation to its surroundings than on the building itself. The whole picture was soon to be more important than its parts. Walpole's first volume of *The Anecdotes of Painting* (1762)[11] includes his brilliant essay on landscape gardening and confirms his love for the subject even though his horizons were limited to the human scale.

So we exchange Walpole's genteel, 'enamelled meadows' for the more rugged stuff of wild mountains, roaring torrents and windswept skies where the ideal building to complete the scene was to remain Gothick.

V

Castles
in the Clouds

ROBERT ADAM, as we have seen, made certain contributions to Strawberry and it was at this time that he was also working on his important Gothick interiors at Alnwick Castle. Earlier in his career many of his Gothick designs, largely unexecuted, show great charm and refinement; but we must also glance at his great castle-style houses that earn him a vital place in the Picturesque. They do not fit comfortably into the Gothick story but, because of their intensely romantic appearance, belong, in spirit, to the earlier phase of picturesque conception. Chronologically they fall into the period of Capability Brown, between Kent and Repton.

The mock castle had even preceded Vanbrugh and, long after the need for defence, fortified-looking houses were being built. The carcasses of Lulworth (form 1588) and Ruperra[1] (early seventeenth century) are reflected at Inveraray [52] (from 1746), and the clear-cut planes of Adam's Seton[2] (from 1790) [53] echo those of Bolsover (from 1612), although Adam's plan contains round shapes. Perhaps we have to look no further back than Robert Smythson for eighteenth-century castle inspiration; in addition, by the time Adam was building his later castles, there were many engraved references of antiquities available, making for a certain uniformity. Medieval forms but little detail were used in his castle compositions and it seems that he was searching for a new style, somewhere between classical and medieval. The plans and elevations were usually regular [60] (see p. 90) unless additions were made at later stages and round-topped fan-lights, sash windows and other eighteenth-century refinements pierced the great sheer walls as at Seton. Although, from a distance, the castles are convincing and of fairy-tale quality,[3] they were not based on a sentimental yearning for the past. It was simply that the eighteenth-century architect was patronised by those who still required a traditional, classical house and those who wanted a 'castle' – or a hybrid of the two. Every architect, reluctant or not, was prepared to be a Goth. Wren, Chambers (whose gothicising of Milton Abbey (from 1771) [54] for the mean and disagreeable Lord Milton was a rare departure from his Roman work),[4] Nash and Decimus Burton may be numbered among the reluctant, and a long list of the willing would include Vanbrugh, Kent, Brown (whose massive Tong Castle, Shropshire of 1765 [55] must have inspired Nash's designs for Aqualate Hall of 1808 in not-so-distant Stafford-shire),[5] Keene, Carr, Paine, Wyatt, Smirke, Porden and Barry. Some could endow the style with grace and magic; others produced designs of little merit in order to comply with fashion. It was, simply, as Dr Rowan says, that 'some Georgian proprietors chose to build castles'[6] aiming at the 'power and grandeur' of the baronial style.

For a house to be in castle style it must have battlements and of the vast number of embattled houses that appeared from the sixteenth to the nineteenth centuries one, Clearwell Castle, Gloucestershire of 1727 [56], is a precocious example of Gothick.[7] It is even earlier than Esher Place but entirely different in spirit; it precedes Miller's activities by a full decade and is entirely alien to them. At first glance the formal west front with central block recessed between taller towers might well pass for an ancient house perhaps later gothicised. The plan, too, is familiar, with central hall and main rooms to the left and right. But in its toughness, the toughness of a more barbaric age, it is set apart from all others of its date. As Dr Rowan has observed, 'the idiom is unfamiliar and totally different to the flimsy angularity of contemporary Rococo Gothic; the architecture is assured and convincing.' Clearwell is a fascinating freak and more 'genuine' than anything that was to follow; it is difficult to assess exactly what proclaims it, in fact, to be eighteenth century. It makes Adam's Mellerstain of twenty-five years later look like the Georgian castle it is – a great grim composition of seventeen bays with the battlements and flanking towers of Clearwell on a gigantic scale. Here Adam provides a *resemblance* to earlier architectural forms but which, unlike Clearwell, could never at close quarters be mistaken for the

52 INVERARAY CASTLE, SCOTLAND (from 1746) by William Adam assisted by his sons, John and Robert.

53 SETON CASTLE, SCOTLAND (1790): a formal composition in romantic vein by Robert Adam.

Opposite

56 CLEARWELL CASTLE,
GLOUCESTERSHIRE (1727): a
castellated house by Roger Morris,
the earliest of its type known.

real thing. After the mid eighteenth century we see these castellated compositions, formal or, later, informal, from Adam's Culzean to Smirke's Eastnor, set in magnificent surroundings and it is this romantic, inspired approach to siting that chiefly gives the houses their appeal. Dr Rowan has placed Adam's castles in the illusionary school of thought – a deliberate combination of baronial splendour and contemporary grace and convenience. This deliberate compromise was, Dr Rowan emphasises,

> a subtlety that escaped the later nineteenth-century critics of the style, who could interpret it only in the light of their own architectural situation. But to accuse the Georgian castle of incompetent initiation is merely to misunderstand it. 'Pseudo' and 'bogus' are not epithets of the period, but the accretions of over a century of disfavour, and they could hardly have been understood by the men who built these houses. To them the castles were examples of a style, not instances of a revival.

This could almost equally well apply to the critics of the whole Gothick scene in all its stages of development.

But what of Adam's interiors? Inside the mournful façade of Mellerstain[8] (from 1770) [57] and the great bastion of Culzean[9] (from 1777) [58], we find all the modern requirements of grace and convenience in a series of classical rooms, some in his most dazzling style, Culzean containing a magnificent oval staircase of Roman grandeur – but no Gothick. It relies on its picturesque siting and grouping for its effect [59]. At Mellerstain there is a glimmer of Gothick in the prettily vaulted corridor linking the classical rooms, but no more. We have to conjure up the lost interiors of Alnwick Castle of the 1760s–70s to judge his merit in the idiom.

His patron at Alnwick was Sir Hugh Smithson, first Duke of Northumberland, to whom Adam owed the great commissions of Northumberland House and Syon House. Capability Brown was landscaping the grounds at the time[10] and, as an able Goth, may have been responsible, at least in part, for some of the remarkable buildings that adorn the park. But behind all the Gothick

Opposite

54 (top) MILTON ABBEY, DORSET
(from 1771) by Sir William Chambers.

55 (bottom) TONG CASTLE, SHROP-
SHIRE (1765) by Capability Brown.

schemes to be carried out in the great complex of buildings, brilliantly captured by Canaletto, was the Duke's wife, formerly Lady Elizabeth Seymour, a great heiress and, according to Walpole '. . . that great vulgar Countess'.[11] Vulgar or not, she was also an extremely tenacious and romantic Goth and was, in spite of this bias, perceptive about architectural matters in general. She also enjoyed, along with other eighteenth-century people of imagination, '. . . a scene of glorious horror and terrible delight'.[12] It was largely due to her (and her money) that Alnwick took on its brilliant Rococo Gothick interiors. Until recently they have often been dismissed as some of Adam's least important works but further research and a renewed interest in eighteenth-century Gothick gives them a place almost as high as that of his classical schemes. Others, too, were involved with the intricate remodelling and decorating of the castle and outbuildings – James Paine (from 1754) who designed the magnificent fan-shaped staircase, also destroyed; Capability Brown's work with Adam and later that of Vincent Shepherd. Little documentary evidence survives to define clearly who was responsible for what work, and research and argument continues to this day.[13] Drawings of Adam's work survive at Sir John Soane's Museum and illustration 61 gives some idea of his determination (and presumably that of the determined Duchess) to leave no surface undecorated. He also designed furniture for the castle in Gothick style of which the chair illustrated in [80] is a rare example and more elaborate than furniture that was being produced by Chippendale and others from the mid century [81 to 85].

In 1775 the Duke purchased the ruins of nearby Hulne Priory – a romantic group of medieval buildings, soon transformed into a summer retreat.[14] The exteriors of the new buildings that supplemented the ruins are of a solid, 'Tudor' nature probably by Brown. In contrast the interior of the fifteenth-century Lord's Tower contains one of the most graceful rooms of the period

57 MELLERSTAIN, SCOTLAND (from 1760): Adam's great classical but castellated house.

Opposite

58 (top) CULZEAN CASTLE, SCOTLAND (from 1777) by Adam, exploiting the intensely picturesque qualities of the setting (see plan on p. 90).

59 (bottom) An imaginary castle in a picturesque setting by Adam, realised at Culzean.

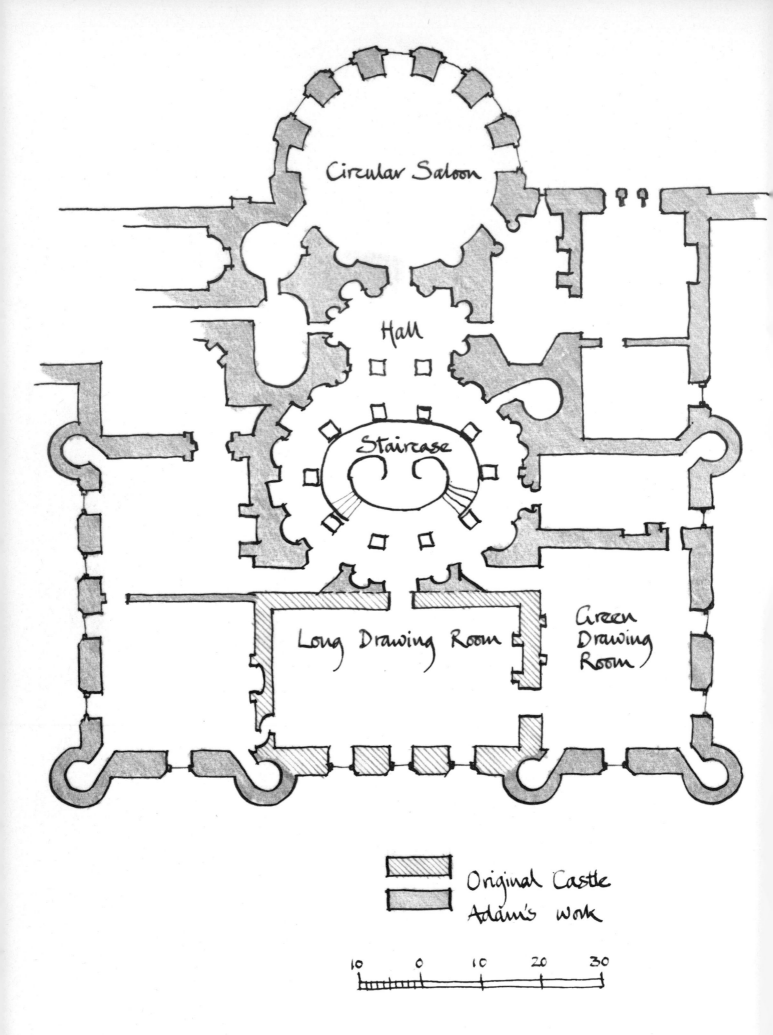

Circular Saloon

Hall

Staircase

Long Drawing Room

Green Drawing Room

Original Castle
Adam's Work

10 0 10 20 30

60 CULZEAN CASTLE: ground floor plan.

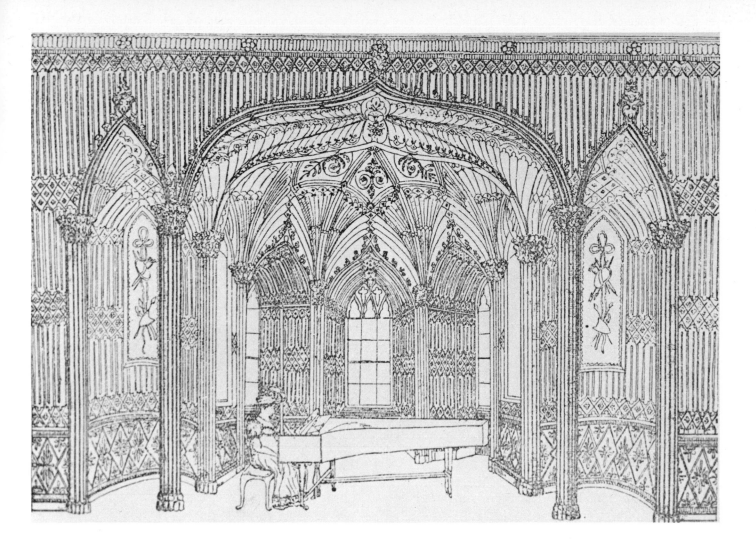

[62] and is almost certainly by Adam. The ceiling is vaulted in a simple manner but the decoration, although only applied to the main features such as the cornice, windows and doors, is of the greatest elegance. Of the same period is Croome d'Abitot Church, Worcestershire [63 and 64] for the Earl of Coventry where Adam and Brown again collaborated, Brown designing the building and Adam decorating the interior. Here again the decoration is confined to the main architectural features as in the church at Preston-on-Stour by Edward Woodward of a decade earlier, Shobdon, Herefordshire[15] [65] of c1750 and Keene's St Mary's Church at Hartwell, Buckinghamshire (1753–6), [66 and 67], four important examples of that great rarity – ecclesiastical Rococo Gothick. The decoration of all four churches would be equally at home in secular buildings and the ceiling at Hartwell, now in ruins in one of England's most affluent counties, would fit perfectly well into any room at Arbury; the unstructural 'Venetian' arches at Shobdon might be found in many a Gothick library.

Another landscape embellishment at Alnwick is the astonishing Brizlee Tower [69], a confection of such originality as to make many other follies such as Wyatt's hideous Broadway Tower of 1797 [68] gauche and dull. Here Adam used Gothick detail as meticulously as he used it indoors and combined it with classical elements of an exotic nature.

Adam's work was destroyed largely by Salvin in 1855, including the most Rococo of chapels, but what we know of his Alnwick Castle does not suggest that Adam was impatient with the idiom, but rather that he was fascinated by its endless possibilities, and no doubt the plasterwork was painted in the familiar pale colours, making his Gothick schemes as delicious as his Roman translations. That he was ignorant of, and perhaps uninterested in, Gothic construction does not detract from his imaginative use of medieval detail in both building and decoration. Few of his designs for Gothick buildings were

63 ST MARY MAGDALEN, CROOME D'ABITOT, WORCESTERSHIRE (1763) by Brown.

Opposite

64 ST MARY MAGDALEN, CROOME D'ABITOT: Adam's decorations for Brown's church.

62 ALNWICK CASTLE: Adam's decorations in the Lord's Tower, an old building in the park probably remodelled by Brown (from 1775).

65 ST JOHN THE EVANGELIST, SHOBDON, HEREFORDSHIRE (1750): the identity of the architect is one of the mysteries of eighteenth-century ecclesiastical building.

66 ST MARY'S CHURCH, HARTWELL, BUCKINGHAMSHIRE (1753–6) by Henry Keene.

67 ST MARY'S CHURCH, HARTWELL: the ceiling before complete decay, probably the work of Robert Moor who collaborated with Keene at Arbury. The interior was a more elaborate version of Keene's earlier remodelling of the chapel at Hartlebury Castle for Bishop Maddox.

68 James Wyatt's neo-Norman tower at Broadway, Worcestershire (1794).

69 ALNWICK CASTLE: the Brizlee
Tower in the park (1777–8), one of
Adam's most exotic creations.

executed but his projects for follies, churches and bridges of the 1740s and
50s show the pleasure he derived from manipulating the arch, pinnacle and
other ancient features.[16] Frail and spidery his designs certainly are, but they
also have that irresistible felicity so brilliantly displayed in his later classical
work. They combine invention, a thoroughness and refinement often lacking
in the Gothick designs of others. Had more of them been executed they would
undoubtedly rank with those of Keene and would be placed second only to
Wyatt. Adam was the greatest decorator of the century and, in Gothick,
Wyatt only outshone him by possessing a deeper historical knowledge of
Gothic construction. All this would have greatly shocked Adam's tutor on
his Grand Tour, the formidable neo-classicist Clérisseau, to whom all Gothic
was heathen, all classicism the ultimate in architectural expression. But we
may assume that part of Adam's determination to succeed in the Gothick or
castle style was due to his increasing rivalry with Wyatt who had already, at
Heveningham in the 1780s, proved that there was little to choose between
their respective virtuoso displays of neo-classical decoration. Towards the
end of the century Wyatt turned increasingly to Gothick and Adam's
answer to that was his romantic castle style, designed to appeal to clients
who wanted the best of both worlds – a picturesque baronial pile and, usually,
a traditionally classical interior.

Although Wyatt's classicism has been dubbed as near-plagiarism of Adam's
work[17] his approach to Gothick was quite different. Unlike the interiors at
Alnwick, even Wyatt's early naïve work of the 1770s could scarcely be called
Rococo. It was not very pretty; it was, in contrast, more severe and bore
more relation, visually, to ancient precedents although structural truth lay
several years ahead. Adam supplied icing-sugar, Wyatt something less sweet
and more convincing. There was no question of plagiarism here. Eastlake
sits on the fence in judging Wyatt's work but now he can be assessed as the
most imaginative gothicist of the late eighteenth and early nineteenth
centuries.

One of his earliest houses was Lee Priory, Kent, of 1782 [71] for Thomas Barrett, friend and correspondent of Walpole who became emotionally enthusiastic about it. It was, he said, '. . . a child of Strawberry, prettier than the parent, and so executed and finished'.[18] This was, of course, great praise from Walpole and the house was, if not pretty by today's meaning of the word, exceptionally original. An older, 'queer old mansion'[19] had existed on the site, part of which was retained but his design for the new house[20] was revolutionary in several respects, the most spectacular room being the library on the first floor which was octagonal in shape and lit by a galleried lantern crowned by a spire, the most dominant and eccentric exterior feature. Inside the lantern was carried on a dome of blind tracery which in turn was supported on clustered columns dividing the walls at intervals into arched recesses containing bookshelves. Walpole's Closet, similar in some respects, was incidental to the plan at Strawberry; at Lee, Wyatt exploited the idea and made it the central feature.

The general appearance of the house was to give the impression of a monastic foundation and the word 'priory' was invented to fortify this illusion and was, says Mr Dale, 'so decked out in fancy dress that lovers of Gothic thought it had the real flavour of the genuine article'.[21] Lee was far more sophisticated than his first Gothick essay, Sheffield Place, Sussex, of only some six years earlier. Here we have a basically Georgian house decorated with pinnacles and battlements, mostly rendered in cement and, like Sandleford Priory in Berkshire is a classical house in disguise. Sheffield Place[22] is set in Capability Brown's marvellous landscaping of 1776 and its interior contains some distinguished and strange features. Like most of Wyatt's early Gothic work, the interiors are decorated with either medieval

71 LEE PRIORY, KENT (1782–90): an early Gothick house by James Wyatt, demolished in 1954.

Drawn by J.P.Neale.

Engraved by T.Barber.

LEE PRIORY,
(SOUTH WEST VIEW.)
KENT.

Printed by J & G.Bishop.

Proof

London. Pub. Jan. 1.1826 by J.P.Neale.16. Bennett St. Blackfriars Road & Sherwood, Jones & C? Paternoster Row.

or classical detail and occasionally a room will contain a glimmer of both idioms. The double-return staircase [72 and 73] is of some splendour, classical in conception but Gothick in detail. The slim wood balusters (every fourth one, in fact, being of undetectable iron) carry the eye gently to the gallery above in a composition of great elegance reminding us of Chute's design at Donnington Grove of 1760. The main bedroom has a most skilfully painted ceiling[23] with a deep cove containing garlanded figures of lions, tigers and leopards. The bed of the ceiling is divided into panels, two painted with playful cherubs surrounded, as is the central rose feature, with festoons of ivy. The predominant colour is pink, the style classical but a hint of Gothick is seen in the *trompe-l'oeil* fan vaults at each angle of the cove.

Wyatt, born in Tamworth, Staffordshire, in 1746, the sixth of seven sons, was the most celebrated and prolific member of a family to be prominent in architecture and the arts for over a century. He fell between two stools, missing the Langley-Miller period of random use of medieval detail and dying before the goths became too seriously immersed in authenticity. He belongs, like Adam, to the age of Romanticism and the Picturesque in both date and in his appreciation of ancient grouping, and takes us over the turn of the century. His rivalry with Adam has already been noted and he carried this even to the extent of designing romantic castles – Shoebury (1797) (unexecuted), Norris, Isle of Wight (1799) and Pennsylvania, Isle of Portland (1800). In 1776 he had been appointed Surveyor to Westminster Abbey in succession to Keene after which he carried out his controversial alterations and restorations to the cathedrals of Salisbury, Lichfield, Hereford and Durham. This work was severely condemned by John Carter[24] and other antiquaries, including Milner whose *Dissertation on the Modern Style of Altering Ancient Cathedrals . . .* (1798) savagely attacks Wyatt's predilection for clearing aisles and chapels of old monuments in order to gain uncluttered views of the interiors. But his romantic castles owe their existence to his later appointment, in succession to Sir William Chambers, as Surveyor General of the Works in 1796 involving work at Windsor Castle, part of which he renovated. Mr John Harris notes that the substance for his three castles came from Windsor – from Chambers's Queen's Lodging of 1777, and Hugh May's work in the Upper Ward of the seventeenth century.[25]

Wyatt's official appointments therefore, brought him into contact with some of the most important medieval buildings in England and he was, as at Windsor, able to examine the work of others who had employed a medieval style. With this experience his own Gothick buildings became increasingly competent and, in a sense, the more competent they became the duller were the results. His last great Gothick composition, Ashridge [74 and 75] in Hertfordshire (1803–13)[26] for the tiresome seventh Earl of Bridgwater, is a solemn, rambling affair far removed from fantasy but reflecting his greater knowledge of medieval design and construction. 'It was in fact,' says Mr Dale 'a serious Gothic building, seriously conceived and seriously executed . . .'[27] His earlier, naïve houses have more appeal, free as they were from pedantry.

Wyatt's whole career was blighted by an inability to concentrate on one client long enough to complete a job without untold misery on both sides. His personal life was often in turmoil, his work always the subject of controversy and his death in a road accident at the age of sixty-seven deprived him of his appointment as Surveyor-General and Comptroller of Works, a position where he might have distinguished himself in the field of public works and planning. Nevertheless his output was prodigious and there was never a moment when he was not in demand. His greatest classical work, Heveningham Hall, Suffolk,[28] (1788–99) was not completed when he had already embarked on the greatest Gothick house of the century – Fonthill Abbey [76 and 77]. It is somewhat of a wonder that Fonthill was ever built and today it is difficult to believe that it ever existed. His client, William

Beckford, was even more erratic and unreliable than he was, but somehow they survived a series of disasters and quarrels to produce the most extraordinary building in Europe. 'I do not drink,' said Beckford, 'I build.'[29] Wyatt did both.

As Strawberry and Fonthill, although separated in conception by over fifty years, are the two most important Gothick houses of their times, the personalities of their owners should in some degree be compared. As we have seen, Walpole possessed unattractive qualities but he was also gregarious, optimistic and almost always happy with his Twickenham toy. At Strawberry Walpole lived a life of happiness tinged with sadness. At Fonthill sadness predominated and Beckford was forever in a ferment over the building of the house, leading the life of a sour, pessimistic pederast behind the twelve-foot-high walls of his estate. His more sympathetic qualities are less easy to find. Both had great imagination and original literary ability, Beckford's *Vathek* (1786) being the answer to Walpole's *Otranto*; both were acquisitive and enthusiastic in embellishing their houses. But there, in broad outline, the similarity between these dilettanti arch-goths must end and their houses turned out to be as different as their characters. Strawberry gave pleasure to Walpole and his friends and Fonthill stood, for its brief life, as solitary and forlorn as its creator. Beckford was too exotic a bird to thrive in the English social climate and except when very young, abroad or in Bath in old age, remained behind his walls. Walpole compromised and probably because of a lack of any lasting intimate attachment chose to flourish in society and the rewards of friendship.

The story of the building of Fonthill is as well documented as that of Strawberry,[30] and begins with Beckford's increasing distaste for Fonthill House[31] where he was brought up as heir to a fortune in West Indian sugar plantations. His early obsession with the romance of the Orient (he wrote *Vathek* at the age of twenty-two) inflamed this distaste for a house so tied to classical tradition and we might have expected him to anticipate Sezincote or the Royal Pavilion and raise a domed tribute to Xanadu. But the melancholy aspects of Gothic images obviously suited his domestic ideals better than the bright, gaudy splendours of the East; these were reserved for his famous novel. In his correspondence he sometimes yearns for sunshine, but he loved the shadows more. He got nearer than anyone to producing this Gothick gloom, an atmosphere wrecked only by his choice of rich, colourful fabrics and the glitter of his avidly hoarded art treasures. The style also provided, as it did for so many, a more suitable setting for the display of family arms in stained glass and plaster.

Wyatt was called in at an early stage – when Beckford was thinking in terms of a building that would serve as a summer retreat for picnics, and as a picturesque object in the landscape when viewed from Fonthill House. It was to be a great tower incorporated in what was to appear to be the ruins of an ancient convent. There was no question of living there permanently and probably just as well, for Wyatt's plaster tower collapsed and in 1805 Beckford in a rare moment of optimism commissioned him again, this time to transform the retreat into a vast house and shrine for himself and his ever-increasing number of possessions. The tower collapsed again in a storm before Beckford moved in and a third tower, this time of stone, hastily replaced it.

During the building of the Abbey, however, Beckford and his household somehow managed to live there, lending even more fantasy to a scene already charged with the improbable. The members of the household and those concerned with the building were, in Beckford's imagination, all extraordinary and all were given nicknames. Beckford's pet dwarf, to his amusement once found huddled and terrified in the dog-basket under the stairs during a thunderstorm, was known as 'Nanibus', his land steward 'The Great Dolt', his valet 'Mme Bion', Samuel Rogers, the poet (one of the few people allowed

72 SHEFFIELD PLACE, SUSSEX (*c*1778) by Wyatt. The staircase leading to the domed gallery.

73 SHEFFIELD PLACE: the staircase landing with classical use of medieval ornament.

to visit the house) 'The Yellow One', Westmacott, the sculptor, 'Rhinoceros', Beckford's dog 'Viscount Fartleberry' and he nicknamed himself 'Barzaba' in his correspondence when referring to his pederastic pursuits. Wyatt did not escape and was known as 'Bagasse' (whoremonger)[32] but, in keeping with Beckford's uneven temperament and the architect's fecklessness, Wyatt was either completely in favour or completely out of it. '. . . tell Bagasse not to renew again his treacheries and negligencies. Oh, my shame, oh my blushes . . .! Am I to suffer this traitor again?' he writes in self-indulgent frustration. But when things are going well he records a few weeks later: 'My dear, angelic, most p-p-p-p-perfect Bagasse is killing himself with work; every hour, every moment, he adds some new beauty.'[33]

Against this bizarre background and with his own contrary nature with which to contend, Wyatt somehow built the most fantastic house to date and Beckford's own descriptions of frantic work being carried out by flares at night still makes exciting reading:

> It's really stupendous, the spectacle here at night, the number of people at work, lit up by lads; the inummerable torches suspended everywhere, the immense and endless spaces, the gulph below; above the gigantic spider's web of scaffolding – especially when, standing under the finished and numberless arches of the galleries, I listen to the reverberating voices in the stillness of the night, and see immense buckets of plaster and water ascending, as if they were drawn up from the bowels of a mine, amid shouts from subterranean depths, oaths from Hell itself . . .[34]

Later peacocks strutted on the new lawns and the dwarf opened the enormous Gothick doors to reveal the shortlived splendours within.

The centre of the plan [77] was a great octagon [79] with its famous and ill-fated tower from which spread four vast wings only the north and south

74 ASHRIDGE, HERTFORDSHIRE (1808–13) by Wyatt, completed after his death by Jeffry Wyatt.

75 ASHRIDGE: the staircase in the great hall.

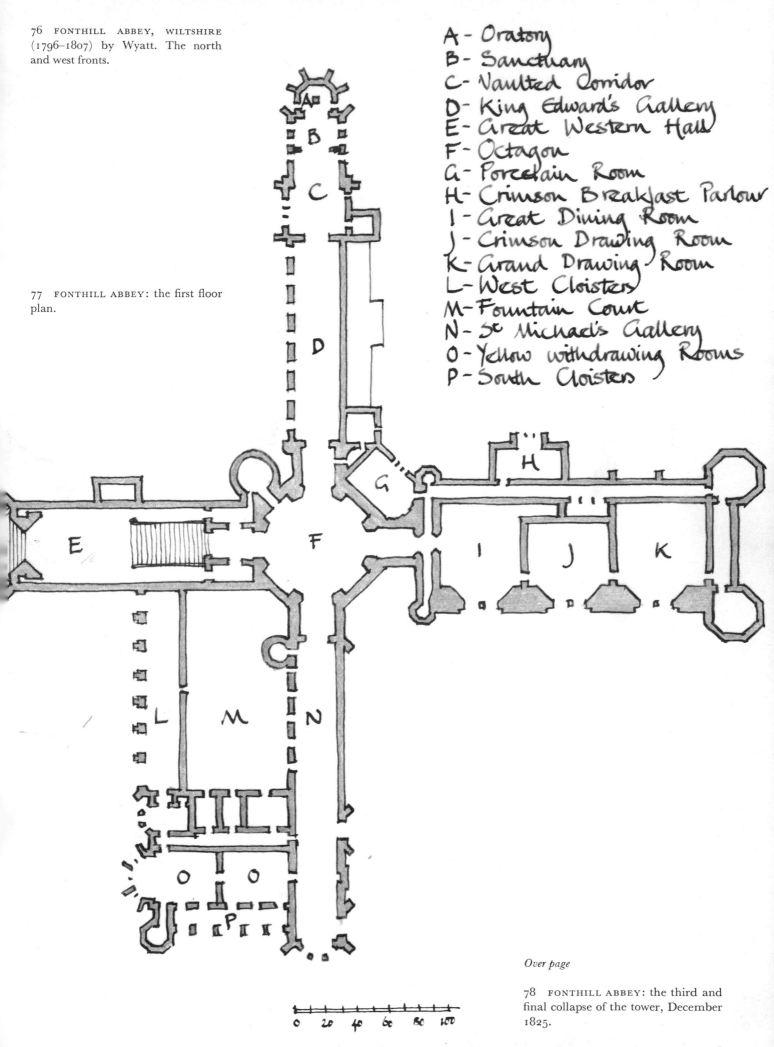

76 FONTHILL ABBEY, WILTSHIRE (1796–1807) by Wyatt. The north and west fronts.

77 FONTHILL ABBEY: the first floor plan.

A – Oratory
B – Sanctuary
C – Vaulted Corridor
D – King Edward's Gallery
E – Great Western Hall
F – Octagon
G – Porcelain Room
H – Crimson Breakfast Parlour
I – Great Dining Room
J – Crimson Drawing Room
K – Grand Drawing Room
L – West Cloisters
M – Fountain Court
N – St Michael's Gallery
O – Yellow withdrawing Rooms
P – South Cloisters

Over page

78 FONTHILL ABBEY: the third and final collapse of the tower, December 1825.

0   20   40   60   80   100

of which were roughly similar, containing, on the main floor, two long galleries – King Edward's to the north and St Michael's, over 100 feet in length, to the south. The west wing contained the main entrance – the great western hall – with its broad staircase leading to the octagon or grand saloon. The east wing, wider than the others, contained the great dining-room, the crimson drawing-room and the grand drawing-room. Of the three floors, the ground mainly contained offices screened by 'cloisters' to the south west which were seen when approaching from the south to enter the great western hall. The second floor of the south wing, however, reveals another side of Beckford's nature – that of the simple recluse with a bedroom of spartan deprivation over the great oriel windows of St Michael's gallery. Other rooms in the wing were, it must be admitted, less spartan, with a library forty-four feet in length filled with rare books on travel, topography and allied subjects leading to the chintz boudoir containing Beckford's more personal treasures. But these rooms and others on this floor were more intimate and private than the vast vaulted chambers on the floor below, crammed with yet more antiques, paintings, ceramics and other works of art. They were a refuge from the ostentation and the outward show born of emotional insecurity. He dreaded to be alone in the Abbey even for a single night, his love of the melancholy being purely romantic and hateful in practice.

The great western hall was designed as a refectory, Nelson being entertained there in 1800, but as it could not be heated the idea was abandoned. A staircase replaced the fireplace and it became the awe-inspiring, theatrical progress to the octagon, the heart of the Abbey. Engravings make the hall look dull and lacking in originality with its imitation oak hammer-beam roof seventy-eight feet above the foot of the stairs carrying heraldic shields, but John Rutter's description[35] makes it sound splendid enough. Viewing it from the staircase, Rutter treats it as a foreground to the great western avenue composed not, as in previous generations, of any one species of tree but a mixture of many different ones producing a less formal effect in keeping with the general picturesque character of the newly landscaped grounds.

> The majestic descent of the broad steps, and their arched parapets; the lofty wainscoting and the pointed arches of the walls, filled with the most beautiful glazing, or hidden by crimson draperies, or retiring into a recess which sculpture has dignified with the effigy of a great man;[36] the darkly coloured and elaborately framed roof, displaying in its ample frieze the emblazoned shields of a distinguished ancestry, with all its minutest and most common parts moulded, and arranged into ornamental forms; the massive piers of the Great Portal pierced to give light and access to the staircase within them; and the grand contour of the noble archway, which the gigantic doors seem waiting to close up forever, – all contrast powerfully with the light, the freshness, and the depth of the 'marble air' and the delicate colouring and simple outline of the external scene.[37]

Before he goes into more detail about the decoration and contents of the Hall he ends his general introduction by returning to the staircase to

> . . . ascend leisurely the spacious steps, watching the gradual development of an architecture, which, from the stateliness of its parts, the masterly arrangement of the chiaroscuro, the atmosphere of the coloured light, and the solemn brilliance of the windows, produces an effect very little removed from the sublime.

The vast scale of the hall was undoubtedly its main attraction but it was the arrangement of the rooms on the first floor beyond that gave the Abbey its greatest moments. Never before had a main saloon been the centre of four magnificent internal vistas; nowhere in the world existed a domestic

80 Chair designed by Adam for Alnwick Castle (*c* 1760).

81 A Gothick chair originally at Strawberry Hill (1760s).

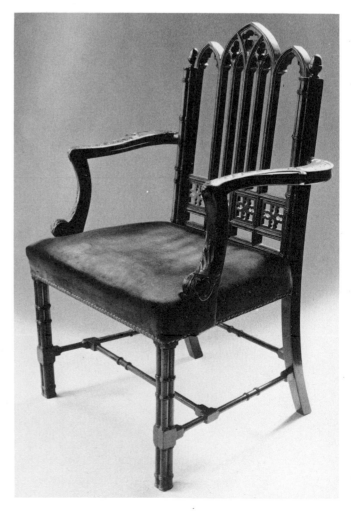

82 A mid eighteenth-century mahogany settee.

85 A mid eighteenth-century yew chair.

83 and 84 Two mid eighteenth-century mahogany chairs.

interior with columns ninety feet high supporting a vaulted ceiling, making a total height of 120 feet. Behind an open arched gallery below the vaulting were sitting rooms connected to bedrooms known as the 'Nunneries'. Originally intended as the chapel, the octagonal saloon was the first Gothick room with the proportions of a cathedral and although the detail was not directly copied from any complete source, it looked authentic and showed Wyatt's increased knowledge of medieval structure. Its authentic look made it, in spite of its astonishing scale, duller than the work of 'the Pest of Strawberry Hill',[38] less magical by far than the icing sugar of Arbury and less sympathetic than any of Wyatt's earlier Gothick houses. Like his work at Belvoir, Windsor and Ashridge his expertise in the idiom was beginning to banish the delights of spontaneity.

That the Abbey was grotesquely unpractical for day-to-day living does not detract from the grandeur of its conception for which the credit must go to Beckford, Wyatt merely carrying out his wishes and producing designs for his client's consideration. The result was bound to be a compromise owing to the fact that rooms intended for occasional use were adapted for permanent living but these aspects apart, the internal vistas alone testified to

86 A mid eighteenth-century
mahogany china cupboard. There is a
less elegant variation on this design at
the Victoria & Albert Museum.

EATON HALL: the saloon where Porden reluctantly used blue as the main colour on the instructions of his client, the second Earl Grosvenor.

Beckford's brilliant imagination and would undoubtedly have found favour with Edmund Burke, author of the influential *Inquiry into the Origin of Our Ideas of the Sublime and the Beautiful* (1756). St Michael's Gallery was 112 feet in length from the octagon to a great oriel window in the south and was also the main library. Although over twice the size, it was Beckford's answer to Walpole's gallery, but the plaster fan-vaulting was simpler and the total effect less fussy. The most astonishing vista of all was from the oriel to the oratory at the northern end of King Edward's gallery, over 300 feet in length and linked by the octagon. King Edward's gallery was so named because of Beckford's descent from Edward III whose portrait hung over the chimney-piece. The stained glass in pointed windows in the west wall contained the arms of seventy-two Knights of the Garter from whom Beckford also claimed descent, which were repeated in a deep plaster frieze round the room. The elaborately carved oak ceiling and heavy oak furniture, the centre table bearing special treasures, helped to give the gallery a decidedly Tudor air. In both galleries the predominant colour was that of the crimson carpets, wall-coverings and curtains, the latter combined with deep blue. The sanctuary and oratory were connected by the vaulted corridor of oak with gold enrichments where, according to Rutter, 'an involuntary silence falls upon every visitor'. Up one step was the sanctuary and the five-sided oratory 'where the walls are covered with damask of the richest dye, where columns, spreading into fans, and shooting their mouldings over the vault, develops a network of burnished gold over our heads – such is the enchantment which prevails, that an indescribable feeling of quietness and contentment steals upon the mind'. It was here that Beckford placed an alabaster statue of St Anthony of Padua on an altar flanked by silver-gilt candelabra containing thirty-six candles and where the memory of the wordly trappings in the preceding treasure-laden rooms was intended to fade.

The second floor of this wing contained the State Bedroom, the Tribune room (overlooking the octagon) and a narrow room known as the Lancaster Gallery. The east wing containing the dining-room and drawing-rooms was never finished and was still being built when Wyatt died in 1813. It was here that Beckford hung his favourite pictures and built the Porcelain Room connecting the east and north wings.

Having glimpsed something of Fonthill's interior we must now consider a more important aspect – its place in the history of the landscape – for it is a building in relation to its surroundings that forms the theme of the last phase of Gothick. Here Beckford's visual romanticism was at its peak and in much of his correspondence he shows an almost violent attachment to the splendours and terrors of Nature. He made his avenue 100 feet wide and over a mile long and much other of the planning and planting was on this monumental scale. Unlike Walpole, he loved the challenge of wild, untamed landscapes. 'I know nothing more powerful than your sketch of those alpine crags, immense oaks and profound deeps, those leafy abysses, impenetrable to the wind, out of which rise the ruins of the ancient castle. It must be imposing, it must speak to the soul' he wrote[39] in 1811 in a moment of romantic enthusiasm. And he tried to capture something of this atmosphere when landscaping the relatively rolling but bleak contours of the Wiltshire Downs. The highest point was Stop's Beacon and below this Beckford devised his wonderfully varied informal gardens bordering the broad lawns on which the Abbey stood. Each had its own particular character; an American plantation was formed and filled with azaleas and rhododendrons;[40] a Norwegian lawn was surrounded by firs and a pinetum planted; an Alpine garden was constructed out of the quarry used for building the house and a large artificial lake was filled with wildfowl. Much of his knowledge of gardening and landscaping was derived from his travels in Portugal where he became passionately devoted to the dramatic surroundings of Cintra. During the first year alone he estimated that he planted one million trees, the majority of them firs of various kinds adding to the 'alpine monastery' effect he desired.

Every aspect of the building in relation to its surroundings was given the most meticulous thought and nothing was planted that would not seem to have been once part of a great forest, a clearing made simply for building the Abbey!

There it stood, a consummate exercise in grand scenic effect, its tower visible for miles around until it collapsed for the last time in 1825, three years after Beckford had sold the estate and retired to Bath. In architectural history Fonthill assumes the part of the sinister villain of the piece, influencing few other buildings except Hadlow Castle [122] the folly in Kent of 1840, and, as Sir John Summerson has remarked, the plan of the Houses of Parliament. It was also the most extravagant monument to Romanticism but, even with all Beckford's efforts, fits uncomfortably into the pictorial ideal, failing, because of its great height, to merge with the landscape and its interior paying more homage to the Sublime than to the Picturesque.

And perhaps it is fitting that little or nothing stands of this marvel and that it should remain, like 'Vathek', in the imagination. 'It seems,' said Beckford 'that they believe in Fonthill as blindly as in pious times they believed in the most inconceivable legends.'[41]

VI

The
Perfect Picture

A VISUAL AWARENESS of the value of picturesque groupings had been appreciated by architects, landscape gardeners and writers since the beginning of the eighteenth century when, in 1709, Vanbrugh saw that the ruins of Woodstock Manor, if retained, would enhance the landscape of Blenheim Palace and Christopher Hussey's 'essay on a way of seeing'[1] is the classic dissertation on the subject. The paintings of certain seventeenth-century Italian and French artists – Salvator Rosa, Claude Lorrain, Gaspar and Nicolas Poussin – became an inspiration to those who were to see nature as a series of pictures and, as already noted, Kent was the first actually to arrange his surroundings like a painting. Capability Brown did likewise in his own manner but it was Humphry Repton who got nearer to the ideals of The Picturesque of the 1790s when the Movement was substantiated by Sir Uvedale Price's *Essays on the Picturesque . . .* (1794–8) and Richard Payne Knight's poem 'The Landscape' (1794) and his *Analytical Inquiry in the Principles of Taste* (1805). These publications, together with Repton's *Sketches and Hints on Landscape Gardening* (1794) had enormous influence on the appearance of the landscape and its buildings and the Picturesque dominated the scene well into the nineteenth century, spreading to the Continent in the form of 'le jardin anglais'. It was a movement that, over the years, had developed beyond Burke's *Inquiry . . .* (1756), through Brown's now detested creed, into a practical philosophy opening the eyes of everyone to the possibilities of combining house and grounds into a complete picture – nature being made to imitate a painting.

Richard Payne Knight introduces us to John Nash, the great name in Regency architecture, for it was on the Welsh borders at the end of the eighteenth century that this erudite squire of Downton Castle, Herefordshire (1774) [87], and friend of Price met the ambitious architect when he was exiled there after a bankruptcy scandal in London. Through them Nash met Repton with whom he entered a partnership more, as it turned out, to the benefit of Nash than to Repton. Soon to become the Prince Regent's favourite, Nash learnt very quickly the importance of being able to supply a Gothick house in picturesque surroundings although his career started as classicist under the wing of Sir Robert Taylor. His first known Gothick house was, like Midford Castle, in Somerset (*c* 1775) [88] more in the nature of a folly, in the tradition of Blaise Castle, Bristol (1766), Racton Tower, Sussex (1770) and Haldon Belvedere in Devon (1788) [89] and other triangular buildings before and after it. It was called Castle House [90] and was built for Price in *c*1792 on the once romantic, rugged cliffs of Aberystwyth. Soon he was to combine house and garden into one picturesque whole, Repton designing the garden and Nash the inevitable Gothick house. His detail was poor and he rarely went to original sources for his patterns; but the general effect of the irregular outline was sufficient to create the desired balance between nature and art. As Dr Crook puts it: 'The Rococo began, and the Picturesque completed, the conjunction of architecture with nature.'[2] Even Nash's classical scenes in Regent's Park were picturesque – the great plaster 'palaces' being varied in style, size and scale and the landscaped park, like that of St James's Park to follow, as informal as is possible to imagine. Gothick designs obviously bothered Nash enough for him to make his famous remark that 'one gothic window costs more trouble in designing than two houses ought to do',[3] this in spite of building East Cowes Castle, across the Solent from that gem of follies, Luttrell's Tower of *c*1780 [91]. Most of his best Gothick houses are more interesting than his classical ones and he was, in any case, able to delegate the boring detail work to A. C. de Pugin, his assistant, and father of A. W. N. Pugin, himself to become a father of the Gothic Revival. Nash's short-lived interiors of 1814 at Carlton House for the Prince Regent were his most lavish Gothick designs, competing in their own bizarre manner with the oriental splendours he created at the Royal Pavilion.

87 DOWNTON CASTLE, HEREFORD-
SHIRE (1774) by Richard Payne
Knight, exponent of The Picturesque
and author of *The Landscape* (1794).
The house links Strawberry Hill with
the castle-style houses of John Nash,
who may also have contributed to the
design.

Downton was a great influence on Nash and he may have worked later
there himself. It was irregular in plan and outline by design and additions
which were subsequently made only increased its romantic qualities. It was
an object lesson in asymmetry and embraced all the tenets of the Picturesque.
It was a mock castle with a classical interior, as several of Nash's were to be,
and the beauty of the plan was that it could be extended in any direction only
adding to the variety of its silhouette. He knocked his castles into a neat
formula, using some of the features of Downton – the towers linked by lower
blocks and also open loggia-cloisters usually with a balcony above to join his
round and square towers, as we see at West Grinstead Park, Sussex (*c*1806)
[92]. He also applied this formula to his Italianate houses of Cronkhill and
Sandridge.[4] It was convenient, picturesquely irregular and allowed for endless permutations of plan, the towers sometimes forming a bay to a main
room [98], sometimes containing a circular room and, as in his own East
Cowes Castle (from 1798) [93], a circular staircase [94] (see p. 131). The
loggia was, of course, not a new linking device and had come from Italy; it
had been used at Hatfield and elsewhere, to join symmetrical towers and later
at Arbury in a formal façade, but Nash took a lead from Walpole and used his
loggias to link disparate features, an element soon to be inherited by many
builders of early nineteenth-century castle-style houses. In Ireland we can
trace the progress of Gothick from the early and schizophrenic Castle Ward

88 MIDFORD CASTLE, SOMERSET (1780s): a folly and house combined, possibly by John Carter.

89 HALDON BELVEDERE, DEVON (1778): perhaps the most perfect of all follies, its stark, dramatic exterior containing rooms with lavish Gothick plasterwork.

with classical and Gothick fronts of 1765[5] [95], via Luttrellstown (1800), Charleville Forest (from 1800) [96] which Mr Mark Girouard has called 'perhaps the finest Gothic Revival house in Ireland',[6] Nash's Killymoon of 1802 [97], his Lough Cutra of 1811[7] and the Dunsany Castle interiors of the 1780s.[8] Many of these were late eighteenth- or early nineteenth-century additions to earlier houses. Few Gothick castles were built on virgin sites, most of them incorporating the remains of earlier buildings. The early nineteenth century also saw an increasing number of classical houses being given a Gothick shroud and many a plain, unfashionable, classical box was transformed by a jumble of towers, turrets and battlements, one of the few recorded graphically being Hawarden Castle, Flintshire where a drawing of 1809 [99] shows the classical house somewhat reluctantly submitting to its medieval mantle by Thomas Cundy, the elder.[9]

90 CASTLE HOUSE, ABERYSTWYTH (c1792): Nash's first known essay in Gothick, long since demolished.

In the Isle of Wight it was much the same story and there were good groups of mock-castles and new Gothick houses on more modest scales. We have already noted Wyatt's work here but over the island were scattered houses of much character, mostly now, alas, gone, such as Fern Hill [100] with its spectacular double-story verandah reminding us of an Indian palace, Lord Vernon's castellated 'Tudor' mansion and many other whimsical creations in great variety. In architecture the Picturesque period became a 'free-for-all' battle, bringing stylistic chaos – the period of the Royal Pavilion, Sezincote, Cockerell's Moorish-Hindu fantasy and of Gothick used with dashes of 'Monastic', 'Chinese', 'Egyptian', 'Romanesque' and mixtures of all or any. Such exotic overtones were originally invented for the few seeking novelty (as was the Chinese of Claydon of the 1770s) but, like those using Gothick before Walpole, 'the few' became many, and, with the help of numerous

91 LUTTRELL'S TOWER, EAGLE-
HURST, HAMPSHIRE (*c*1780): a model
castellated folly on the Solent.

92 WEST GRINSTEAD PARK, SUSSEX (*c*1806): one of Nash's 'standard' castle-style houses.

93 EAST COWES CASTLE, ISLE OF WIGHT (from 1798): Nash's own house, where he entertained his patron, the Prince Regent, and to which he added over a number of years and where he died in 1835.

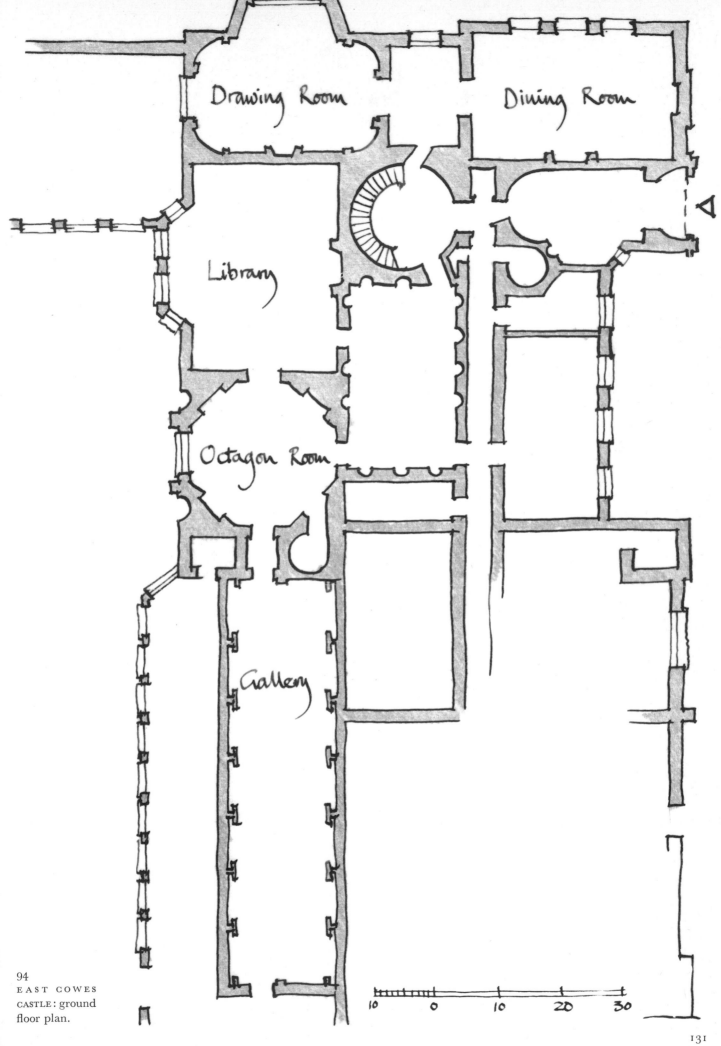

Drawing Room

Dining Room

Library

Octagon Room

Gallery

94
EAST COWES
CASTLE: ground
floor plan.

95 CASTLE WARD, CO. DOWN (1765): a classically-disposed Gothick façade. Later Nash was to build several Gothick houses in Ireland but all in irregular, romantic style.

96 CHARLEVILLE FOREST (from 1800): the plasterwork is of high quality but less sumptuous than that at Arbury.

publications, no builder was at a loss to provide the most outlandish designs, the text often carefully calculated to inflame a vernacular already charged with gross snobbery. It was Andrew George Cook who in 1790 produced a book with the explicit title: *The New Builder's Magazine, and Complete Architectural Library, for Architects, Surveyors, Carpenters, Masons, Bricklayers, etc. as well as for Every Gentleman who would wish to be a Competent Judge of the Elegant and Necessary Art of Building . . .* and so on until *The whole forming a complete System of Architecture in all its Branches, and so disposed as to render the Surveyor, Carpenter, Bricklayer, Mason, etc. equally capable to erect a Cathedral, a Mansion, a Temple, or a Rural Cot.* The operative word here is 'system' and although the author thought that a secular building should be classical and an ecclesiastical Gothick, he nevertheless offers some whimsical Gothick designs and those in the 'Fancy Style' for the occasional house, garden embellishments and other trivial conceits.

Other books devoted to country house design (there were over thirty published between 1780–1815)[10] many of which contained sententious and patronising generalities, didactic rules for trivial subjects and snobbish illusions to the class of person to whom the book was addressed. Thus Robert Lugar's *Sketches* (1805)[11] are suitable to 'persons of Genteel Life and moderate fortune' but, George Richardson makes no bones about the fact that his 'extensive and costly designs'[12] were aimed at 'gentlemen of fortune' as Richard Elsam writes for the 'Nobility and Gentry'.[13] But there were many shades in between ranging from James Peacock (who was also 'Jose MacPacke' author of *Nutshells* of 1785, a sharp and influential paper), long-time assistant to George Dance, the younger, who wrote for 'gentlemen of Moderate fortunes' and suggested that any builder could construct one of his designs from plan only, using any elevation that appealed to the owner. Sir John Soane produced a book for labouring-class dwellings,[14] but this was an age when, in general, well-established architects did not publish their designs as did their eighteenth-century counterparts. It was an age when unestablished architects could best proclaim their wares by producing books or pamphlets of designs accompanied by their own pet theories on style, suitability for purpose, materials and surroundings. Much of the text is as fantastic as some of the designs themselves, many of which never saw the light of day but only added to the chaos already created by lack of stylistic discipline. But the books clearly indicate the new trend in architectural practice, a trend towards providing the lower income groups with a tinge of what their social superiors already possessed, and abound with those overworked and conflicting qualities of 'elegance', 'simplicity', 'variety', 'uniformity', 'beauty', 'utility', 'convenience' and 'economy'. But it is in T. D. W. Dearn's *Architectural Sketches* (1805) that much is made of convenience and economy – the obvious way in which to appeal to the new class of house-builder who also still wanted the security of being in fashion. In other words, architecture was now 'packaged' and the styles from which to choose were all set out in these attractively illustrated books. Much of it was Gothick, and aimed at those rising on the tide of the Industrial Revolution. In 1823 Dearn published *Sketches in Architecture . . .* several of the designs being aimed hopefully at owners of large estates requiring buildings for servants and tenants [101 and 102].

But whilst the demand for Cook's 'Rural Cot' rose, there were no signs that the upper classes were rejecting his ambitious ideas for 'cathedrals' for secular purposes. Vast cathedral-like mansions rose from the beginning of the nineteenth century, one of the most startling being Eaton Hall, Cheshire (from 1803), by William Porden for the second Earl Grosvenor. It was what Eastlake considered 'one of the most important attempts at Pointed architecture'[15] and, although essentially an essay in picturesque 'Tudor Perpendicular' is almost symmetrical in plan [103]. Its vast, daunting, prickly exterior [104] must have been, when completed in 1825, the most remarkable

97 KILLYMOON CASTLE, CO.
TYRONE (1802): one of Nash's most
successful small houses, containing an
ingeniously planned interior.

Regency house in England and the interior was of a sumptuousness fitting for
its owner and knew no bounds in luxury and extravagance. It was a decorator's
paradise and Porden was responsible for its realisation from the elaborately
vaulted ceilings to the furnishings and furniture. There was much stained
glass in Strawberry-Fonthill style but the general impression of the interiors,
if one can rely upon the Bucklers' watercolours engraved as a series in
1826,[16] is one of brilliant colours – of walls, carpets, curtains and other
furnishings as sumptuous as those at the Royal Pavilion. It was rare for a
whole house to be completely furnished in Gothick style but such was the
case at Eaton. Unfortunately little of Porden's furniture survives, two
examples being the chairs designed for the Hall and those for the Saloon
(see p. 120). With the publication of many more books on cabinet-making
the middle-class market was, by the early nineteenth century, flooded with

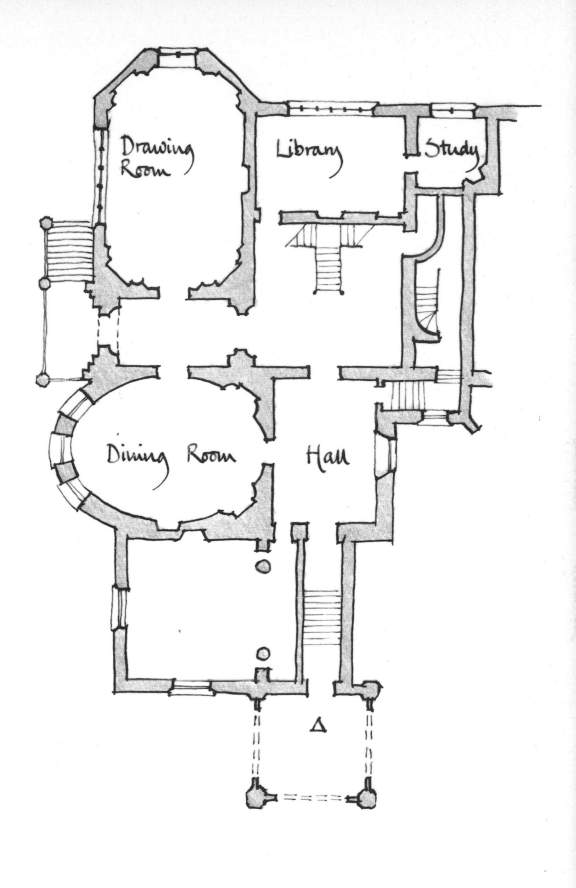

Drawing
Room

Library

Study

Dining Room

Hall

10   0   10   20   30

98 KILLYMOON CASTLE: ground floor plan.

Hawarden Castle
October 20. 1809.

99 (above) HAWARDEN CASTLE,
FLINTSHIRE (from 1809): a classical
house receiving a Gothick face-lift.
Nash proposed a grander remodelling.

100 (left) FERN HILL, ISLE OF
WIGHT (c1820): built for the Duke
of Bolton when governor of the island,
and one of many exotic villas that
have now disappeared.

101 T. D. W. Dearn's design for 'a
small house in the florid Gothic style',
intended to be suitable for a noble-
man's steward (1823).

Plate 6.

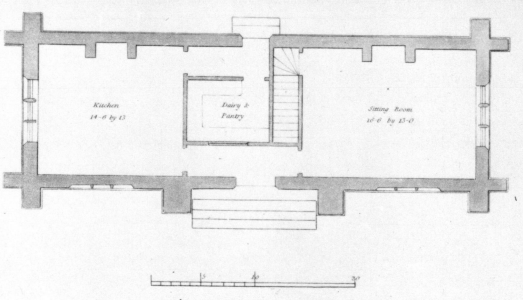

Kitchen
14-6 by 13

Dairy &
Pantry

Sitting Room
16-6 by 13-0

London, Published by J. Taylor, 59, High Holborn.

102 A design by Dearn for 'two dwellings to show as one building' (1823).

Gothick furniture and objects such as lanterns, clocks and other household goods. But the furniture and fittings in the Gothick taste at Eaton were outside such mass-production and were, as befitted such an illustrious patron, pieces of the highest quality made for particular rooms [105 and 106], in contrast to most earlier Gothick furniture which was regarded as a fashionable novelty and used more often than not in a classical setting. For exterior and interior cohesion no other Gothick house rivalled Porden's dedicated masterpiece. Even the great piles of Smirke such as Eastnor Castle, Herefordshire (1812–15) and Lowther Castle, Westmorland (1812–15) [107], the vast Tudor complex of Harlaxton Manor, Lincolnshire, by Anthony Salvin (from 1831), or his more modest Mamhead in Devon (1827–33), the amateur idealism of Charles Hanbury-Tracy's staggering array of towers and pinnacles – Toddington Manor, Gloucestershire (from 1819) [108], Sir William Wilkins's great transformation of Tregothan, Cornwall in 1816–18, could not compete with the magnificence of Eaton. Even Wyatt had made a dull thing of Belvoir (1800–13) by comparison. Many other large Tudor-Gothick mansions were later to rise in Scotland and Ireland from Sir Walter Scott's Abbotsford (1822) to Thomastown Castle, Co. Tipperary (c1820)[17] – all foretastes of heavy, High Victorian castles to come. But the 'Tudor' of Salvin was rapidly taking the place of the Gothick of Wyatt and Nash. Many were to be poor imitations of Salvin's work on a gigantic scale and soon amounted to little more than ostentatious monuments to wealth.

Church architecture, too, was in disarray by this time and we should now return to some of the churches that had been built after the carefree days of Hartwell, Croome and Shobden. It was not until some thirty years later than these sophisticated Rococo churches that we see the charm and elegance of Stapleford Church (1783) by George Richardson,[18] although there were many elegant little Gothick churches erected in between, especially in the Gothick-fertile Midlands, such as William Baker's at Stone, Staffordshire of 1754,[19] and Norton-by-Galby, Leicestershire by Wing of 1770[20] – both 'authentic' and serious interpretations. At Stapleford we see a plain, well-ordered Georgian church [109], all the more charming for its serious attempts at realism and lack of pretension. Still in the Midlands, St Nicholas, Warwick (1748 and 1779–80), is perhaps a more difficult church to appreciate. Its subordinate position for one thing, away from the centre of the town (dominated, as is the countryside, by the great tower of St Mary's) is somewhat unusual for an important Georgian church and its design is strangely unpleasing. Mr Marcus Whiffen has suggested[21] that Miller may have had a hand in the design, but the nave was built during the last year of his life and the tower of 1748 has been ascribed to Thomas Johnson. The nave, almost square, is a curiosity – shallow, widely spread vaulting being supported on six sets of cluster columns on high bases and springing from half-cluster columns in the aisles.

As in secular architecture there are examples of Gothick and classical elements being used together, both in detail of decoration and architectural style. St Paul's Church, Bristol (1789–93), designed by Daniel Hague, presents a dramatically Romantic exterior with its impressive, tall tower [110] but inside, the classical columns supporting a deep ribbed cove and the worldly Adamesque plasterwork over the pointed arch of the choir make ill-assorted, if attractive, features. Among the many late eighteenth-century Gothick churches preceding the great deluge to follow during the Regency period, St Mary's Church, Tetbury (1771–81) [111] remains a perfect example of elegance and daring, Sir John Betjeman calling it 'one of the triumphs of the Gothic Revival'.[22] The slim cluster columns, soon to be used throughout the world in endless cast-iron ranks in churches, conservatories and other buildings requiring decorative support, lead us gracefully to the simple, plaster fan-vaulting. It is frail and theatrical and indeed, as Lord Clark has observed,[23] the plan is that of a theatre, the side-aisles taking the form of exterior cloisters. Tetbury crowns the modestly successful Gothick career of Francis Hiorn and, lovely though it is, it unfortunately heralds hundreds of duller, less exciting Gothick churches to rise throughout the country during the succeeding fifty years or so.

Apart from 214 Church Building Act (1818) churches erected from 1818–33 (of which 174 could be called Gothick) by architects who were not only household names like Nash, Soane and Smirke, the three Attached Architects,[24] the work of one lesser-known man – Thomas Rickman (1776–1841) – stands out as exceptionally interesting. He was not a reluctant Goth but a whole-heartedly willing one and we owe to him (and his brilliant pupil Henry Hutchinson) the 'Bridge of Sighs', St John's College, Cambridge of 1827 [112] and the great, romantic scenery of New Court (1827–31) in late Perpendicular style [113], which provides such a magnificent backcloth to the vast, green sweep of the college lawns. But, also, because he was born into the surge of the Industrial Revolution and great trade and population expansion, he catered for those who now lived in the growing suburbs of the manufacturing towns and for them he built over fifty brand new Gothick churches, mostly in the Liverpool and Birmingham areas.[25] His researches into Gothic entailed, it is said, the examination of 3,000 ecclesiastical buildings,[26] the result of which was his classic work on the various types of Gothic architecture: *An Attempt to Discriminate the Styles of English Architecture from the Conquest to the Reformation* (1817). Here he divided the styles into 'Norman', 'Early English', 'Decorated', and 'Perpendicular' and his treatise became the standard reference until the end of the century by which time it had reached seven editions. Perhaps his most important, and certainly his most inventive, contributions to architecture were the three cast-iron churches of Liverpool where the hard, unsympathetic quality of iron replaced the traditional, soft qualities of stone in both construction and decorative detail. Long before Rickman's time, cast iron had been used for supporting galleries but his aim at Liverpool was different, involving the use of iron for the entire framework, including buttresses.[27] It was to be both revolutionary and influential, Porden using it at Eccleston Church in 1809 and in the Eaton Hall window tracery, and it meant that an elegance even greater than that of Tetbury could be achieved. But its inevitable hardness was not missed by contemporary critics one of whom, J. A. Picton, described Rickman's cast-iron pinnacled St Philips', Liverpool (1816) [114] as a 'feeble imitation of

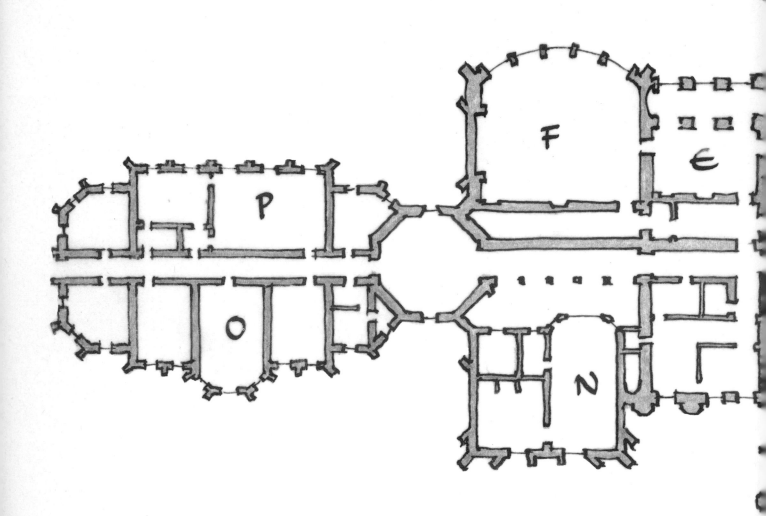

103   EATON HALL: ground floor plan.

A. Portico
B. Entrance Hall
C. Saloon
D. Cloisters
E. Billiard Room
F. Dining Room
G. Ante Room
H. Drawing Room

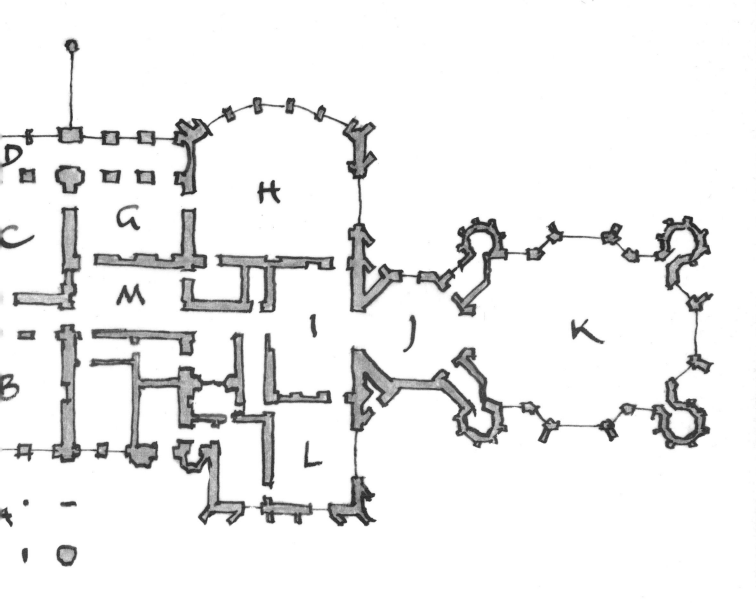

I. Library,
J. Library Octagon
K. Library
L. Morning Room
M. Great Stairs
N. Kitchens
O. Chapel
P. State Bedroom Suite.

Over page

104 EATON HALL, CHESHIRE (from 1803): William Porden's great 'Pointed' composition which defied the fashion for asymmetry.

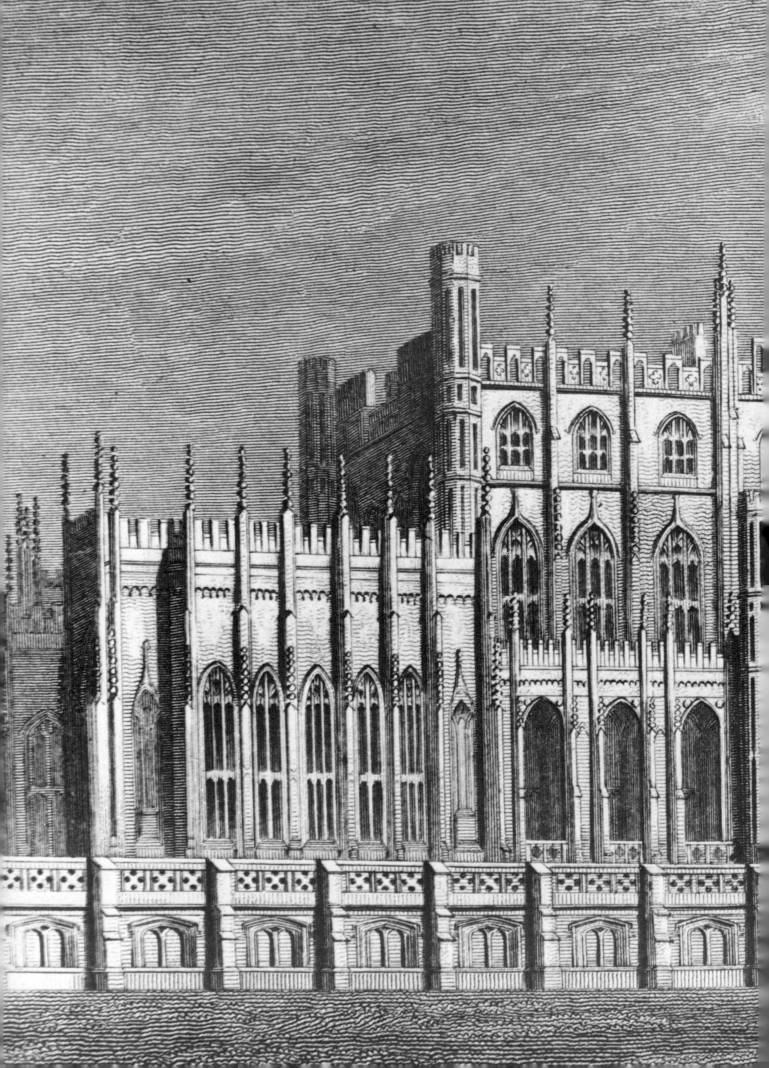

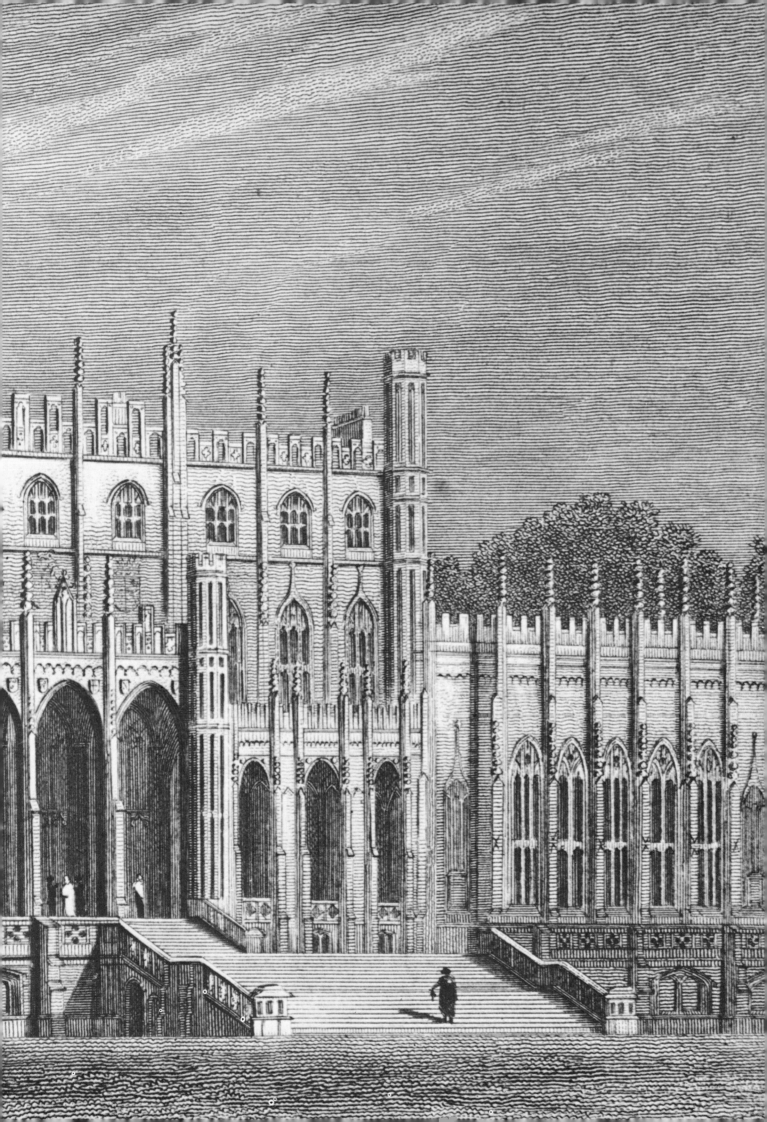

Opposite

107 (top) LOWTHER CASTLE, WESTMORLAND (1812–15): Sir Robert Smirke's formal, classically disposed composition.

108 (bottom) TODDINGTON MANOR, GLOUCESTERSHIRE (from 1819): the Gothick dream of Charles Hanbury-Tracy.

105 (above) EATON HALL: one of Porden's chairs designed for the saloon, seen in the illustration on p. 120.

106 (right) EATON HALL: an oak chair by Porden for the entrance hall.

109 ST MARY MAGDALENE, STAPLE-
FORD, LEICESTERSHIRE (1783):
George Richardson's neat and convinc-
ing interpretation of a Gothic church.
The interior contains very simple
Gothick plasterwork.

110 ST PAUL'S CHURCH, BRISTOL
(1789–93): a dramatic and romantic
composition by Daniel Hague.

King's College Chapel', as stiff and as unbending as the material of which it was built. The other two celebrated iron churches, St George's (1814) and St Michael's (1813–15) (the former being Rickman's first executed design), were equally disliked because of the harshness of the material. His St George's, Birmingham (1820–22) [115] in Pointed style was only criticised by Eastlake on account of its iron tracery. Rickman was at the height of his career when Nash built his 'ridiculous, cheap'[28] St Mary's, Haggerston, London in 1826.[29]

As we have seen, Nash was a successful, if reluctant secular gothicist but like his pupil Decimus Burton (1800–81), unsuccessful in Gothick ecclesiastical work and for opposite reasons; Nash's Gothick churches were usually weak and half-hearted, whereas his pupil's were clumsy and gauche. Burton's father, James Burton, the builder, lived near Tonbridge at Mabledon, a

112 ST JOHN'S COLLEGE, CAMBRIDGE: the Bridge of Sighs, the imaginative design of Thomas Rickman and Henry Hutchinson (1827).

111 ST MARY'S CHURCH, TETBURY, GLOUCESTERSHIRE (1777-81): Francis Hiorn's elegant church, a landmark in Georgian Gothick.

113 ST JOHN'S COLLEGE, CAMBRIDGE: New Court of 1827–31 by Rickman.

114 (above) ST PHILIP'S CHURCH, LIVERPOOL (1816): one of Rickman's celebrated iron churches, based on King's College Chapel.

115 (left) ST GEORGE'S CHURCH, BIRMINGHAM (1820–22), by Rickman. The tracery is of iron, scorned by Eastlake who otherwise liked the design which he called 'late Middle Pointed'.

Opposite

116 (top) MABLEDON, TONBRIDGE, KENT (1805): built for the father of Decimus Burton who later greatly enlarged it for the banking Deacon family. Old stone was used in the building.

117 (bottom) HOLY TRINITY CHURCH, TUNBRIDGE WELLS, KENT (c1827): one of Decimus Burton's heavy attempts at the Decorated style.

tough-looking Gothick mansion of 1805 [116] and his son worked extensively in nearby Kent and Sussex towns. His church at Tunbridge Wells [117] makes an imposing sight from a distance and dominates the surrounding townscape but should not be examined in detail. He was at heart a classicist, as his Hyde Park Corner screen and Regent's Park houses demonstrate, and few of his medieval compositions bear inspection or delight the eye.

Chiefly because of his best-known work, St Luke's, Chelsea (from 1820) [118] the name of James Savage (1779–1853) has a secure place in the history of Gothick. St Luke's is remarkable for its spectacular and genuine stone-vaulted roof – the first to replace the plaster of Rococo and often considered the first church of the Gothic Revival because of its structural honesty. Eastlake, however, makes very heavy weather of this skeletal, attenuated composition which today seems remarkably sophisticated:

> The want of proportion is eminently noticeable in the lanky arches of the west porch, with their abrupt ogival hood moulding; in the buttresses, which are divided by their 'set-offs' into two long and *equal* heights; in the windows, which are identical in general outline throughout the church; in the octagonal turrets of the tower, where the nine string courses occur at scrupulously regular intervals all the way up; and, finally, in the masonry of the walls, where large blocks of stone are used in un-interrupted courses, scarcely varying in height from base to parapet. All these accidents combine not only to deprive the building of scale but to give it a cold and *machine* made look.[30]

His observations are mostly correct and certainly there is a lack of softness and pliability found in the use of materials in medieval building but the result is effective if eccentric. What Eastlake hated most of all was the traditional, formal, Georgian plan but, after much more severe criticism of the interior, he concedes that the groining of the nave is good by comparison with the demon – decorative plaster vaulting. Once more he is incapable of appreciating a building *for what it is*, especially if it pre-dates Pugin. In recent times Lord Clark has described the church as having 'something distinguished in its slim tower, something almost exciting in its perverse flying buttresses. But the building suffers from that meagreness of construction that we notice at Tetbury and which gives a cardboard look to almost all Gothic churches of the time . . .';[31] Dr Crook calls it 'that strangely unimpressive building'.[32]

We must end this brief look at Regency ecclesiastical Gothick with a pre-eminently successful exponent – Charles Barry (1795–1860) – who was to design the greatest Gothick building in Europe, for which he was knighted. Barry built four large Gothick churches, the most successful being St Peter's Church, Brighton [119] of 1824, which makes such a welcome contrast to the classical plaster terraces when leaving Brighton for London. He also invented his own form of Italianate house, his inspiration culled from his travels abroad, partly with Eastlake. But it is, of course, for his Houses of Parliament that his name is immortal – a complex that is beyond the scope of this essay, the enormously intricate detail of which was designed by A. W. N. Pugin (1812–52), arch-critic of all that Gothick stood for. The time had come to dismiss practically all church building of the new century up to 1830 and Pugin, John Britton and his relentless partner E. W. Brayley carried on a continual vendetta against non-structural Gothick, lack of accuracy or any tendency to ignore the strictest rules of archaeology – all essential ingredients of ecclesiological Victorian Gothic. Religious revivals would merge with architecture; liturgy and archaeology were to be synonymous. 'It was,' remarks Dr Crook, 'the triumph of archaeology over romanticism.'[33]

When, however, the Commissioners' rather unsatisfactory churches were rising, the congregations, comprising the rapidly expanding middle-class

118 ST LUKE'S CHURCH, CHELSEA (from 1820) by James Savage, sometimes considered the first church of the Gothic Revival owing to its stone vaulted roof.

119 ST PETER'S CHURCH, BRIGHTON (1824): one of four large Gothick churches by Sir Charles Barry.

communities, were being housed very prettily indeed, often in Gothick villas of beguiling character. The last of the many handbooks already noted took us up to 1815, but a human dynamo was to ensure that a remaining flicker of Romantic ideals would linger on well into the reign of the Gothic Revival. He was John Claudius Loudon (1783–1843), a Scotsman whose first passion was for horticulture and agriculture. He became one of the most remarkable cyclopedists of all time, his *Encyclopaedia of Agriculture* appearing in 1825 and his *Encyclopaedia of Plants* in 1829. But here we are more concerned with his monumental *Encyclopaedia of Cottage, Farm and Villa Architecture and Furniture* (1833) running to over one thousand pages of text and illustrations [120 and 121]. It is a tome of baffling contradictions and contains contributions for those requiring a 'blueprint' for a large mansion to the humblest lodge – the latter often Lilliputian versions of large mansions. The range was great and included designs for furniture, ironwork and fittings for public houses. Its influence was as great as its range and represents 'the transition from the serene graces of the Georgian period to the chaotic romanticism of the Victorian age' as Mr John Gloag, his biographer, remarks.[34] He was equally at home with the classical or Gothic idiom but the *Encyclopaedia* includes numerous variations on Gothick themes, some discussed in Mr Gloag's chapter 'Pageant of Styles' in which he also labels a castellated villa for a small family as 'commercial Gothick'. Loudon also offers many examples of Tudor-style mansions and villas, more pale shadows of Salvin, usually now to be known as being in the 'Old English Style'. If Nash provided the first garden suburb – the Park Villages in Regent's Park (from 1830) – Loudon provided sufficient designs to ensure the future of suburbia itself for ever. His *Encyclopaedia* was published two years before Nash's death. Loudon's classical semi-detached villas in Bayswater (1825)[35] became models for many thousands to form the suburbs of industrial cities and in 1838 he published *The Suburban Gardener and Villa Companion* which brought Repton-style gardening within the reach of every householder. One of his most prolific contributors was Edward Buckton Lamb (1806–69) who could design anything from a pinnacled bed to a large villa containing a 'medieval' library.[36] Lamb, who

120 Design for a circular stable block by Barry for J. C. Loudon's *Encyclopaedia* . . . (1833). He supplied an alternative classical design.

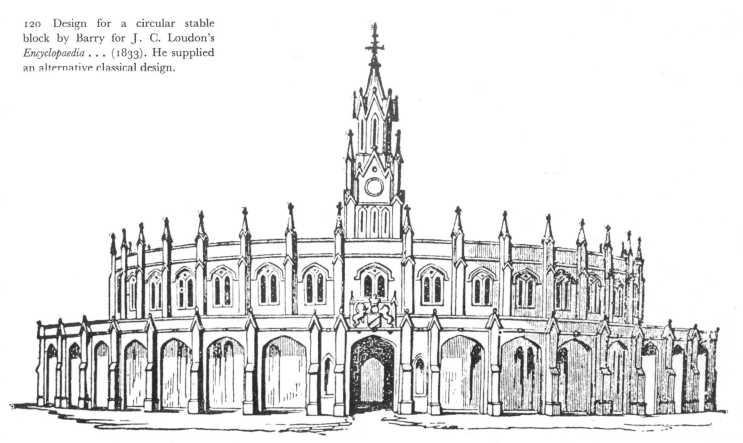

121 (left) Design for a Gothick library by E. B. Lamb for Loudon's *Encyclopaedia* . . . (1833).

122 HADLOW CASTLE, KENT (1840): all that remains of a large mansion of 1830 to which the tower was added later – a final salute to Fonthill and the Picturesque.

appears to have been ignored deliberately by Eastlake, was an able architect of eccentric tastes and also became a chief illustrator for the *Encyclopaedia*. Thus Loudon permeates Victorian England with the last dying embers of the Picturesque and, in turn, Andrew Jackson Downing (1815–52), much influenced by Loudon, spread a similar gospel over the face of North America, its effect lasting for even longer. In the 1840s Alexander Jackson Davis (1803–92) was building Lyndhurst at Tarrytown, New York, an exceptional house of the Gothic Revival but with distinctly Gothick overtones. But in England, this was the end. Ecclesiology had finally won the day and in 1841 *The Ecclesiologist* declared that 'stucco and painting are not out of place in the theatre or ballroom; but in God's house everything should be real'. There was nothing more to be said; the 'k' of Gothick had gone for ever and with it the innocent pleasures of plaster and paint. Structural honesty was to mean more than exotic trimmings, art would not be allowed to cover functional deficiencies and decoration would be limited to a seemly, disciplined pattern. Ecclesiology, combined with a new liturgical fervour, destroyed the sentimental approach to architecture; ruins and decay, inciting the emotions of pleasure and fear, were to vanish. The cold light of reality was replacing the moonshine of fantasy and there would be few left by the mid nineteenth century to heed that familiar voice from Strawberry echoing down the years:

I think there is no wisdom comparable to that of exchanging the realities of life for dreams. Old castles, old histories, and the babble of old people, make one live back into the centuries, that cannot disappoint one. One holds fast and surely what is past.[37]

Notes

Bibliography

Index

Notes

CHAPTER I

1 *Duchess of Malfi* first performed *c* 1613, published 1623.
2 From 'Pollio, an Elegy', written in the wood near Roslin Castle, 1762.
3 From 'Elegy', 1770.
4 Mario Praz, *The Romantic Agony* (1933).
5 'The Ruined Abbey in the Forest', from Ann Radcliffe, *The Romance in the Forest* (1791).
6 There are variations of this poem. See R. W. Ketton-Cremer, *Thomas Gray* (1955).
7 For descriptions see Barbara Jones, *Follies and Grottoes* (1953). See also Hugh Honour, 'An Epic of Ruin-building', *Country Life* (10 December 1953).
8 From *Poems Chiefly Pastoral* (1766).
9 *The Gentleman's Magazine*, published from 1 January 1731, was a great source of contemporary thought on architectural topics and from 1800 the majority of illustrations were Gothic.
10 H. M. Colvin, *A Biographical Dictionary of English Architects, 1660–1840* (1954).
11 See also Charles L. Eastlake, *A History of the Gothic Revival* (1872); edited and with a new introduction and bibliography by J. Mordaunt Crook, Leicester, 1970.
12 Kenneth Clark, *The Gothic Revival* (1928; reprinted 1950, 1970).
13 The building is shown on a map of 1778 signed by Brown. The builder, Sir Christopher Sykes, also corresponded with Carr on the matter. I am grateful to Mr Tatton Sykes for this information.
14 *Ferme Ornée or Rural Improvements* (1800).
15 Eastlake, op cit.
16 Clark, op cit.
17 H. M. Colvin, 'Gothic Survival and Gothick Revival', *Architectural Review* (March 1948). See also J. Mordaunt Crook, 'Northumbrian Gothick', the Alfred Bossom Lecture, University of Newcastle upon Tyne, 13 November 1972, reprinted in the *Journal of the Royal Society of Arts* (April 1973).
18 Thomas Love Peacock, *Nightmare Abbey* (1818).
19 Clark, op cit.

CHAPTER II

1 John Summerson, *Architecture in Britain* (1953).
2 David Watkin, *Thomas Hope and the Neo-classical Idea* (1968).
3 Laurence Whistler, *Sir John Vanbrugh, Architect and Dramatist* (1938).
4 For a description of the park, see James Lees-Milne, *Earls of Creation* (1962).
5 Barbara Jones, op cit.
6 Kerry Downes, *Hawksmoor* (1959).

7 See Michael Gibbon, 'A Manifesto in Ironstone', *Country Life* (10 June 1972).
8 Summerson, op cit.
9 Lees-Milne, op cit.
10 Some of Kent's drawings are at the Victoria & Albert Museum and show a strong Italian, perhaps Venetian, influence. Walpole despised them for their poor perspective.
11 Dorothy Stroud, *Capability Brown* (1950).
12 Horace Walpole, 'On Modern Gardening', in *The Works of Horatio Walpole,* vol II (1798).
13 For Lt General James Dormer.
14 For a description of Kent's work at Rousham see Margaret Jourdain, *The Work of William Kent* (1948). See also Christopher Hussey, 'Rousham, Oxfordshire', in *English Country Houses: Early Georgian, 1715–60* (1955).
15 Joseph Addison had already criticised formal garden planning in his *Remarks on Several Parts of Italy* (1705). See also Miles Hadfield, 'Climax of England's Formal Gardens', *Country Life* (21 June 1973).
16 Clark, op cit.
17 See J. Lindus Forge, 'Kentissime', *Architectural Review* (September 1949).
18 First issued in 1741 as *Ancient Architecture Restored and Improved by a Great Variety of Grand and Useful Designs (1st Part) . . .*', reissued with an essay 'On the Principle Ancient Buildings in this Kingdom', and entitled *Gothic Architecture Restored and Improved . . .* (1742). Langley had already issued a pattern book for craftsmen in 1740 entitled *The City and Country Builder's and Workman's Treasury of Designs.*
19 By T. F. Pritchard for John Johnes of Hafod. Life at Croft Castle is evocatively conveyed in *Peacocks in Paradise* (1950) by Elizabeth Inglis-Jones. See also Arthur Oswald, 'Croft Castle, Herefordshire', *Country Life* (28 April and 5 May 1950).
20 For Sir John St Aubyn, architect unknown.
21 See James Lees-Milne, 'Stout's Hill . . . Gloucestershire', *Country Life* (5 July 1973).
22 *Gothic Architecture Decorated. Consisting of a Large Collection of Temples, Banqueting, Summer and Green Houses; Gazebos, Alcoves; Faced, Garden and Umbrello'd Seats; Terminaris, and Rustic Garden Seats; Rout Houses, and Hermitages for Summer and Winter; Obelisks, Pyramids etc . . .* (1759, reprinted 1968).
23 See Nikolaus Pevsner, 'Good King James's Gothic', *Architectural Review* (February 1950).

CHAPTER III

1 See Lilian Dickens and Mary Stanton, *An Eighteenth-century Correspondence* (1910).
2 See James Lees-Milne, 'Hartlebury Castle Revisited', *Country Life* (23 September 1971).
3 William Shenstone, *Letters*, edited by M. Williams (1939).
4 Christopher Hussey, *The Picturesque* (1927; reprinted 1967).
5 M. Williams, op cit.
6 Known as Shentsone's Chapel; all buildings are now in ruins.
7 *Victoria County History: Oxon*, vol III.
8 See William Hawkes: 'Sanderson Miller', Dissertation for Diploma in Architecture, Jesus College (Cambridge, 1964). See also Anthony C. Wood and William Hawkes, 'Sanderson Miller of Radway and his Work at Wroxton' in *Cake and Cockhorse*, the magazine of the Banbury Historical Society, vol IV, no 6 (1969). The issue contains a list of Miller's works and those attributed to him. For Miller's work at Arbury see also, Christopher Hussey, 'Arbury Hall, Warwickshire', *English Country Houses: Mid-Georgian, 1760–1800* (1956).
9 See Alistair Rowan, 'Gothick Restorations at Raby Castle', *Architectural History*, vol 15 (1972).
10 Warwick County Record Office (CR 764).
11 RIBA Drawings Collection.
12 *Scenes from Clerical Life* (1858).
13 By V. A. Sederbach. See John Britton, vol III *The Beauties of Wiltshire* (three vols, 1801–25) and Rupert Gunnis, *Dictionary of British Sculptors* (1951).
14 See 'Sanderson Miller . . .', in *Cake and Cockhorse*, op cit.
15 See John Cornforth, 'A Countess's London Castle', *Country Life Annual* (1970). See also Hermione Hobhouse, *Lost London* (1971).

16 Warwick County Record Office (125B/584). Letter 30 October 1755.

17 Letters from Miller's family are in Warwick County Record Office and confirm his illness and its nature. I am grateful to Mr William Hawkes for this information.

CHAPTER IV

1 Eastlake, op cit.

2 J. H. Muntz (1727–98), Swiss architect of the long-demolished Gothic Cathedral in Kew Gardens (1759) also joined Walpole for a brief period and made certain contributions to the house.

3 See Christopher Hussey, 'Donnington Grove, Berkshire', *Country Life* (18 and 25 September 1958).

4 R. W. Ketton-Cremer, *Horace Walpole* (1940; reprinted 1946, 1964).

5 Richard Church (*Country Life*, 9 March 1972).

6 Apart from Walpole's *Description of the Villa . . . at Strawberry Hill* (1774), the house appears in numerous topographical guides including N. Pevsner, *Middlesex* (1951), and Christopher Hussey, *English Country Houses: Early Georgian, 1715–60* (1955). For the most recent account see J. Mordaunt Crook, 'Strawberry Hill Revisited', *Country Life* (7, 14, 21 June 1973). The first article reproduces the delicate water-colours by John Carter of 1778 which show how the rooms were decorated and furnished.

7 In fact Walpole quarrelled with Lord Radnor. For a description of this now-vanished Gothick villa with sumptuous classical interiors see *Country Life* (vol LXXXII).

8 Quoted in Clark, op cit.

9 Eastlake, op cit.

10 Walpole succeeded his nephew as 4th Earl in 1791.

11 *Anecdotes* (1762) and other publications were printed on Walpole's own press which he set up at Strawberry in 1757.

CHAPTER V

1 See Mark Girouard, *Robert Smythson* (1966), for illustrations of Lulworth and Ruperra.

2 John Fleming discusses Seton (for Alexander Mackenzie) and its place in Adam's castle-style building in 'A Retrospective View by John Clerk of Edlin . . .' in *Concerning Architecture* (1968).

3 James Malton in his *Designs for Rural Residences* (1802) offers a design for a castle closely resembling Adam's drawing in illustration 60.

4 See John Harris, *Sir William Chambers* (1970).

5 See Stroud, op cit, for an account of Tong, and Terence Davis, *The Architecture of John Nash* (1960) for an illustration of Aqualate.

6 Alistair Rowan, *The Castle Style* (Cambridge PhD Dissertation, 1965).

7 See A. Rowan, 'Clearwell Castle', in *The Country Seat* (1970). Mr Colvin has discovered evidence in the Dunraven Papers (National Library of Wales) that the house was designed by Roger Morris.

8 For George Baillie of Jerviswood.

9 For the 10th Earl of Cassilis.

10 See Stroud, op cit.

11 Walpole, *Correspondence*. To G. Montagu, 23 December 1759.

12 *Diaries of a Duchess*, edited by J. Grieg (1926) and quoted by J. Mordaunt Crook in 'Northumbrian Gothick', op cit, 1972.

13 See A. C. S. Dixon, *The Restoration of Alnwick Castle*, 1750–86, B Arch (Durham University, 1960).

14 See John Fleming, 'Adam Gothick', *The Connoisseur* (October 1958).

15 Various architects have been suggested for this church including Kent, Bentley and Walpole's Robinson. Mr Colvin informs me that Dicky Bateman, nephew of Lord Bateman for whom the church was built, was entrusted with the works but would have engaged a professional architect for the design. Dr Crook has suggested T. F. Pritchard (1723–77) who worked in Gothick at nearby Croft Castle. He would have been about 36 years old at the time.

16 See John Fleming, *Robert Adam and his Circle* (1962), for an account and illustrations of some unexecuted works.

17 See Anthony Dale, *James Wyatt* (1956), for a discourse on the working relations of Wyatt and the Adam brothers. See also James Lees-Milne, *The Age of Adam* (1947).

18 Quoted in Dale, op cit.

19 Eastlake, op cit.

20 Demolished in 1954. The house had been drastically altered by Sir Gilbert Scott in the 1860s. The Strawberry Room is now in the Victoria & Albert Museum. See also Hugh Honour, 'A House of the Gothic Revival', *Country Life* (30 May, 1952).

21 Dale, op cit.

22 For the Lord Sheffield, friend of Gibbon.

23 By Charles Cotton, RA.

24 In his 'Pursuits of Architectural Innovation', *The Gentleman's Magazine* from 1798.

25 John Harris: 'Georgian Country Houses', RIBA Drawings Collection, *Country Life* (1968).

26 The work was completed after Wyatt's death by his nephew, Jeffry Wyatt, later Sir Jeffry Wyatville.

27 Dale, op cit.

28 For Sir Gerard Vanneck, Bt.

29 Beckford to G. F. Franchi, Beckford's closest friend, with whom he kept up a voluminous correspondence. See Boyd Alexander, *Life at Fonthill, 1807–22* (1957).

30 See John Harris, *A Country House Index* (1971), for a list of contemporary books describing Fonthill. Anthony Dale, H. A. N. Brockman, J. W. Oliver, Boyd Alexander, Guy Chapman and Kenneth Clark are some of the many who have written about the house.

31 Also known as 'Splendens'.

32 These nicknames and those of others in Beckford's circle are to be found in Alexander, op cit.

33 Alexander, op cit.

34 Beckford to Franchi; Alexander, op cit.

35 John Rutter, *Delineations of Fonthill and Its Abbey* (1823). Beckford supplied him with most of the basic material.

36 Beckford's father, Alderman William Beckford.

37 Rutter, op cit.

38 Beckford's description of Walpole.

39 To Franchi describing the park at Hamilton Palace.

40 A *Country Life* photograph reproduced in H. A. N. Brockman, *The Caliph of Fonthill* (1956), gives some idea of its landscaping.

41 Alexander, op cit.

CHAPTER VI

1 C. Hussey, op cit. Those who have pursued the subject either for its own sake or in relation to certain exponents include John Summerson, *Architecture in Britain*, op cit; Kenneth Clark, *Landscape into Art* (1946); E. F. Carritt, *A Calendar of English Taste* (1949); Dorothy Stroud, *Capability Brown*, op cit and *Humphry Repton* (1962); David Watkin, *Thomas Hope . . .*', op cit and Nikolaus Pevsner, 'The Genesis of the Picturesque', *Architectural Review* (November 1944). Many other authors have explored various aspects of the Picturesque manifestation and its place in the history of landscape painting, architecture and literature.

2 Eastlake, op cit.

3 Quoted in Clark, op cit.

4 See Davis, op cit for illustrations.

5 Castle Goring, Sussex (c1800) by J. B. Rebecca is another two-faced house.

6 See Mark Girouard, 'Charleville Forest, Co. Offaly', *Country Life* (27 September 1962).

7 See Davis, op cit for illustrations.

8 See John Cornforth, 'Dunsany Castle, Co. Meath', *Country Life* (27 May 1971).

9 See John Cornforth, 'Hawarden Castle, Flintshire', *Country Life* (15 and 29 June 1967).

10 See Sandra Blutman, 'Books of Designs for Country Houses', *Architectural History*, vol II (1968).

11 *Architectural Sketches* (1805).

12 *New Designs in Architecture* (1792); *The First Part of a Complete System of Architecture* (1794) and *New Vitruvius Britannicus* (1802).

13 *An Essay on Rural Architecture* (1803).

14 *Sketches in Architecture* (1793).
15 Eastlake, op cit.
16 See Guy Acloque and John Cornforth, 'The Eternal Gothic of Eaton', *Country Life* (11 and 18 February 1971).
17 See Mark Bence-Jones, 'Thomastown Castle, Co. Tipperary', *Country Life* (22 October 1969).
18 See Marcus Whiffen, *Stuart and Georgian Churches, 1603–1837* (1947–8).
19 See Whiffen, op cit for illustrations.
20 See Whiffen, op cit for illustrations.
21 Whiffen, op cit.
22 *Collins Guide to English Parish Churches* (1958), edited by John Betjeman.
23 Clark, op cit.
24 They produced specimen designs for the Church Commissioners, Nash offering ten designs of which seven were Gothick. See Rhodi Liscombe, 'Economy, Character and Durability: Specimen Designs for the Church Commissioners, 1818', *Architectural History*, vol 13 (1970).
25 See E. D. Colley, *Thomas Rickman*, MA Dissertation, Manchester University (1962).
26 See H. M. Colvin, *A Biographical Dictionary of English Architects*, op cit.
27 See Turpin Bannister, 'The First Iron-framed Buildings', *Architectural Review* (April 1950).
28 John Summerson, *Georgian London* (1945).
29 See Davis, op cit for illustration.
30 Eastlake, op cit.
31 Clark, op cit.
32 Eastlake, op cit.
33 J. Mordaunt Crook, 'John Britton and the Genesis of the Gothic Revival', in *Concerning Architecture* (1968).
34 *Mr Loudon's England* (1970).
35 Nos 3 and 5 Porchester Terrace.
36 See Gloag, op cit for further illustrations.
37 W. S. Lewis, editor of the Yale Edition of Walpole's Correspondence, from 1945. (Walpole to Montagu, 5 January 1766; quoted in Ketton-Cremer, op cit.)

ADDISON, J. *Remarks on Several Parts of Italy* (1705)

ANGUS, W. *The Seats of the Nobility* . . . (1787)

BECKFORD, W. *Vathek* (1786)

BENTHAM, J. *A History of . . . Ely* (1771)

BRITTON, J. *Beauties of England and Wales* (1801–15)

——. *Architectural Antiquities* (1807–26)

BURKE, E. *A Philosophical Enquiry into the Origin of Our Ideas on the Sublime and the Beautiful* (1757)

CARTER, J. *Ancient Architecture of England* (ed J. Britton, 1837)

CHATTERTON, T. 'Elegy' from *Collected Works*, vol I (1770)

CHIPPENDALE, T. *The Gentleman and Cabinet-maker's Directory* (1754)

DEARN, J. D. W. *Sketches in Architecture* (1823)

DECKER, P. *Gothic Architecture* (1759)

DUGDALE, W. *Monasticon* (from 1655)

EASTLAKE, C. L. *A History of the Gothic Revival* (1872)

ELIOT, G. *Scenes from Clerical Life* (1858)

ELSAM, R. *An Essay on Rural Architecture* (1803)

GANDY, J. *Designs for Cottages . . . and Other Rural Buildings* (1805)

——. *The Rural Architect* (1805)

GILPIN, W. *Three Essays on Picturesque Beauty* (1794)

GRAY, T. *Six Poems* (illustrated by R. Bentley, 1752)

GROSE, F. *Antiquities of England and Wales* (1783–7)

HALFPENNY, J. and W. *Chinese and Gothick Architecture Properly Ornamented* (1752)

——. *Rural Architecture in the Gothick Taste* (1752)

INCE and MAYHEW. *A Universal System of Household Furniture* (1762)

KNIGHT, R. P. *The Landscape* (1794)

——. *An Analytical Inquiry into the Principles of Taste* (1805)

LANGLEY, B. and T. *Gothic Architecture Restored and Improved* . . . (1742)

LEWIS, M. G. *The Monk* (1795)

LOUDON, J. C. *Encyclopaedia* . . . (1833)

LUGAR, R. *Architectural Sketches* (1805)

MACPEAKE, J. *Nutshells* (1785)

MASON, W. *English Garden* (1771–81)

MICKLE, W. J. *Pollio* (1762)

MORRIS, F. O. *A Series of Picturesque Views* . . . (undated)

NASH, J. *The Mansions of England in the Olden Time* (from 1839)

NEALE, J. P. *Views of Seats* . . . (1818–29)

PAPWORTH, J. B. *Rural Residences* (1818)

PEACOCK, T. L. *Nightmare Abbey* (1818)

PLAW, J. *Ferme Ornée* (1795)

——. *Sketches for Country Houses* . . . (1800)

——. *Rural Architecture* (1802)

PRICE, U. *An Essay on the Picturesque as Compared with the Sublime and the Beautiful* (1794–8)

PUGIN, A. C. *Specimens of Gothic Architecture* (with E. J. Wilson and J. Britton, 1821–3)

RADCLIFFE, A. *The Mysteries of Udolpho* (1794)

REPTON, H. *Sketches and Hints on Landscape Gardens* (1794)

——. *Fragments on the Theory and Practice of Landscape Gardening* (1816)

RICHARDSON, G. *New Vitruvius Britannicus* (1802)

RICKMAN, T. *An Attempt to Discriminate the Styles of English Architecture* (1819)

RUTTER, J. *A Delineation of Fonthill* . . . (1823)

SHENSTONE, W. *Unconnected Thoughts on Gardening* (1764)

SMITH, G. *The Cabinet-maker's and Upholsterer's Guide* (1826)

SOANE, J. *Sketches in Architecture* (1793)

SPENSER, E. *The Faerie Queen* (illustrated by W. Kent, 1751)

STUKELEY, W. *Itinerarium Curiousum* (1724)

——. *Palaeographia Sacra* (1736)

VARDY, J. *Some Designs of Mr. Inigo Jones and Mr. William Kent* (1774)

WALPOLE, H. *Anecdotes of Painting* (1762)

——. *The Castle of Otranto* (1765)

——. *A Description of . . . Strawberry Hill* (1784)

——. *The Works of Horatio Walpole* (1798)

WARTON, T. *Essays on Gothic Architecture* (with J. Bentham, F. Grose, and J. Milner, 1800)

WEBSTER, J. *The Duchess of Malfi* (1623)

WHATELY, T. *Observations on Modern Gardening* (1770)

WRIGHT, W. *Grotesque Architecture* . . . (1767)

TWENTIETH CENTURY

ALEXANDER, B. *Life at Fonthill, 1807–22* (1957)

——. *England's Wealthiest Son* (1962)

BETJEMAN, J. (ed). *English Parish Churches* (1958)

BROCKMAN, H. A. N. *The Caliph of Fonthill* (1956)

CARRITT, E. F. *A Calendar of English Taste* (1949)

CHAPMAN, G. *Beckford* (1937)

CLARK, K. *The Gothic Revival* (1928)

——. *Landscape into Art* (1946)

COLVIN, H. M. *A Dictionary of English Architects, 1660–1840* (1954)
CROOK, J. M. (ed). *Eastlake: A History of the Gothic Revival* (1970)
DALE, A. *James Wyatt* (1956)
DAVIS, T. *The Architecture of John Nash* (1960)
——. *John Nash, the Prince Regent's Architect* (1966)
DICKENS, L. and STANTON, M. *An 18th-century Correspondence* (1910)
DOWNES, K. *Hawksmoor* (1959)
FLEMING, J. *Robert Adam and his Circle* (1962)
GIROUARD, M. *Robert Smythson . . .* (1966)
——. *English Country Houses: Victorian* (1970)
GLOAG, J. *Mr Loudon's England* (1970)
GRIGSON, G. *The Romantics* (1942)
GUNNIS, R. *Dictionary of British Sculptors, 1600–1851* (1951)
HARRIS, J. *Georgian Country Houses* (1968)
——. *Sir William Chambers* (1970)
——. *A Country House Index* (1971)
HOBHOUSE, H. *Lost London* (1971)
HONOUR, H. *Horace Walpole* (1957)
——. *Chinoiserie* (1961)
HUSSEY, C. *The Picturesque* (1927)
——. *English Country Houses: Early Georgian, 1715–1760* (1955)
——. *English Country Houses: Mid-Georgian, 1760–1800* (1956)
——. *English Country Houses: Late Georgian 1800–1840* (1958)
INGLIS-JONES, E. *Peacocks in Paradise* (1950)
IRWIN, D. *English Neoclassical Art* (1966)
JONES, B. *Follies and Grottoes* (1953)
JOURDAIN, M. *The Work of William Kent* (1948)
——. *English Interior Decoration, 1500–1830* (1950)
KETTON-CREMER, R. W. *Horace Walpole* (1940)
——. *Thomas Gray* (1955)
LEES-MILNE, J. *The Age of Adam* (1947)
——. *Earls of Creation* (1962)
LEWIS, W. S. *Horace Walpole* (1961)
——. *Walpole's Correspondence* (Yale University, from 1945)
LITTLE, B. *James Gibbs* (1955)
MACAULAY, R. *Pleasure of Ruins* (1953)
PEVSNER, N. *The Buildings of England* (from 1951)
PIGGOTT, S. *William Stukeley* (1950)
PILCHER, D. *The Regency Style* (1947)
PRAZ, M. *The Romantic Agony* (1933)
——. *Three Gothic Novels* (edited by P. Fairclough, 1968)
QUENNELL, P. *Romantic England* (1970)
RICKMAN, T. M. *Notes on the Life . . . of Thomas Rickman* (1901)
ROWAN, A. *Garden Buildings* (1968)
SITWELL, S. *British Architects and Craftsmen* (1945)
STEEGMAN, J. *The Rule of Taste* (1936)
STROUD, D. *Capability Brown* (1950)
——. *The Architecture of Sir John Soane* (1961)
——. *Humphry Repton* (1962)
SUMMERSON, J. *John Nash, Architect to King George IV* (1935)
——. *Georgian London* (1945)
——. *Heavenly Mansions* (1949)
——. *Architecture in Britain, 1530–1830* (1953)
TURNOR, R. *The Smaller English House* (1952)
VARMA, D. P. *The Gothic Flame* (1957)
WATKIN, D. *Thomas Hope . . .* (1968)
WHIFFEN, M. *Stuart and Georgian Churches* (1947–8)
WHISTLER, L. *Sir John Vanbrugh* (1938)
——. *The Imagination of Vanbrugh . . .* (1954)
WILLIAMS, M. (ed). *Letters of William Shenstone* (1939)

References to articles in books and journals and to unpublished theses are made in the Notes.

Index